Matting & Framing

THE HOBBYIST'S COMPLETE PICTURE FRAMING BOOK

Matting &
Framing

THE HOBBYIST'S COMPLETE PICTURE FRAMING BOOK

Penelope Angell

DRAKE PUBLISHERS INC.
NEW YORK • LONDON

Published in 1976 by
Drake Publishers, Inc.
801 Second Avenue
New York, N.Y. 10017

LCCN: 76-28313
ISBN: 0-8473-1141-4

Printed in the United States of America.

Table of Contents

Preface

Art plays a vital part in giving a room a finished, balanced appearance. The framing of a work of art has a large bearing on its effectiveness in the eyes of the viewer. Yet professional framing can be quite expensive. This book is written to demonstrate that art can be presented to best advantage in an inexpensive way. The intention here is to offer framing ideas that are *easy, economical* and *based on good design.*

With ease as a main consideration, ready-made frames, framing kits and frame-it-yourself shops are discussed in chapter 3, and several temporary frames are presented in chapter 11. Step by step photographs of all procedures involved in framing art are included. They are intended to make the book easily understood and its suggestions easily followed for beginners as well as those who have previously framed and finished pictures.

Economy is also a consideration in this book. The proposals here use a minimum of equipment and inexpensive materials with alternate suggestions of utensils found in most homes. All proposals and demonstrations are intended to serve as examples of good design.

Although ease may be an important consideration at times, it is to be remembered that the more work done on a frame, the more control on the design so that it will blend with the work of art . . . also the more pleasure can be gained from actually experimenting and doing the work.

Special thanks go to Arnold Spangler who spent many hours helping with demonstrations and offering suggestions. Sincere thanks also go to Larry Taylor, Aluminum Section Frame, Inc.; Betty, Guy, artist; and Boyce Benge, The House of H. Heydenryk, Jr. Inc.

LIST OF ILLUSTRATIONS

Matting & Framing

THE HOBBYIST'S COMPLETE PICTURE FRAMING BOOK

Chapter 1

Framed Art — The Finishing Touch and an Insight into You

So, you've bought the ultimate in artistic creations and you want it to grace your home. Or perhaps there's a wall in your living or dining room that could carry a watercolor or photo grouping quite handsomely. Whether you begin with the art work or the place to hang it, the finishing effect might well tell observers more about you than you think.

Your choice of art can lend your personality to every room of your home. Original paintings, prints, photos and posters can combine with pieces of sculpture and other decorative objects to display your taste, color preference, hobby interests, favored old masters, past travels, friends and family.

One important picture can turn a large wall surface into a focal point of your room. A grand picture centered over the living room sofa, hung at eye level, can complete a striking vignette. An "important picture" however, does not mean one with an elaborate frame. On the contrary, such a frame often detracts from the picture.

A picture grouping can also be a pleasing attraction on a wall. The grouping can be placed symmetrically so that from the center line both sides are mirror images of each other, or the grouping can be asymmetrical (which is often more interesting) with each side balanced from the mid point, but in a somewhat different arrangement.

As you read, you'll become aware of ways of treating your art to best advantage in your setting. You'll become familiar with how frames can complement and serve to enhance a picture. For example, a large, bold, modern graphic might work great wonders in a flat, narrow steel frame. While a print of an old master might look better in an antique frame treated with a coating of raw umber glaze. You'll also learn how to mount, mat, frame and finish your art step by step.

What to Frame and Hang

It might be said that you hang your life's story when you hang a work of art. Your subject, color, textural and material preference, if you've been able to guide the framing and matting of the work, will be on display. All have been evolving as you've been progressing along. It naturally gives you greatest pleasure when those things you hang have been a close part of you—a remembrance, or perhaps art you've created. Your vacation photos, your children's art, a shadow box of your

stamp collection, matches, Christmas cards or letters from friends . . . all can be framed to add your personality to your rooms, and at the same time add an artful touch to your walls.

"What Should I Frame?" There are few limits to what can be framed and displayed attractively with the proper framing technique. But to have a finished product that pleases you, it is wise to start with a plan.

Start with a Method of Attack

First of all, you might place your favorite canvases, prints, and watercolors in the living and dining rooms . . . and reserve the den, family room and informal living room for your snapshots and collections.

Art should relate to the furniture and architectural elements. This does not mean that a mat should be chosen to match the color of sofa upholstery. Choice of the mat should rest entirely on the picture it will surround. It is the picture that should be compatible with the colors in the room.

If you're hanging more than one informal snapshot or family treasure collection for pride and for pleasure, you might consider dividing the art into subjects: family records, family collections and treasures, family artwork. Or divide the snapshots into family holidays, family with friends, or special occasions. If hanging more than one collection in the same room you might want to hang the highest and lowest pictures at the same level—perhaps with the largest or the most elaborate frame in the center and the corners anchored by a medium size picture or two smaller ones in a set. The frames need not match, although only one or two should be elaborate.

NOTE: Before you begin, arrange the pictures on the floor as you like them. Make a sketch and take measurements. Then you're ready to begin hanging your art.

Fig. 1. (Opposite Page) Here is a symmetrical grouping from Greg Copeland of three long, narrow ladies suitably contained in three long, narrow frames—adding up to a whimsical note. The framed block prints on rice paper are by Stephen White.

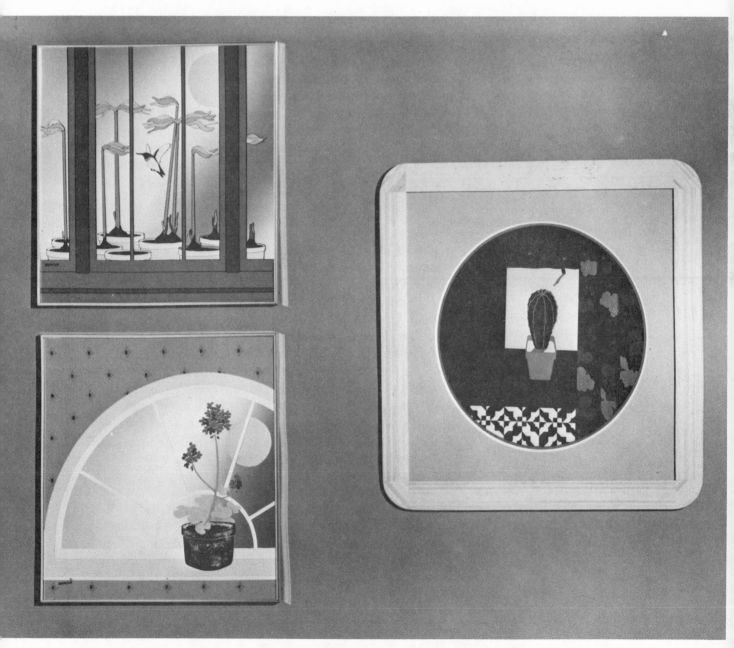

Fig. 2. (Above) The asymmetrical picture grouping on the left, from Greg Copeland, combines two mirror graphics (far left) in brilliant colors, by John Sember, with a serigraph of a potted cactus by Ardith Truhan. Although in different frames and done in different techniques, the pictures seem to balance and hold together.

If your taste runs to modern art, remember that these pictures need lots of space around them. Often, a bold modern painting is the main attraction in its area of the room. Don't worry about tying it down with accessories. What it really needs is room to soar.

As you read these suggestions, do remember that satisfaction comes from art because it is a creative form. Its dynamic quality rests in the fact that any rules or suggestions can be countered to good effect. Experimenting is the key to getting the effect you want, or perhaps to coming across a good effect you hadn't thought of achieving.

Another suggestion—alas, to be broken: on textured walls, or walls with patterned wallpaper, it is often best to hang a subject with a large mat. The mat can separate the picture from the pattern or texture of the wall.

On wood paneling you might want to hang a wide wood frame that is painted or stained a darker color than the paneling. This helps to separate the picture from the wall. The inside edge of the frame next to the picture might be accented with a light line of white or gold, especially if the painting is dark.

Why a Frame?

Let's take a step backward. Surely at some time a frustrated frame hunter on a limited budget has thrown up his hands and wondered if his picture really had to be framed anyway. It's a fair question, but one that could best be answered by anyone who has seen a work of art both before and after it has been framed.

The frame *contains* the art. It limits the boundaries of the art and focuses your vision on the subject. The frame reinforces the picture both aesthetically and as a protective device. It should blend with the style of the art work and be proportionate to it. When you're choosing molding or a finish, remember that the frame is to accommodate the picture. Your choice of frame should be dictated by the subject of the art. It's so easy to be caught up in the various elaborate moldings and finishes that one is apt to lose sight of this fact. It is better to take out your fits of "high fashion" artistry on mirrors than subject a piece of art to an elaborate frame that is unsuited for it.

Generally, a three-dimensional appearing picture looks best in a frame that slants inward. A one-dimensional picture looks best in a flat frame.

Frames serve to protect their subject by separating it from dirt, dust and grease, not to mention fingerprints. The aesthetic and protective purposes of the frames of today are far afield of their original 15th century use which was to support paintings as portable units. Inserts such as mounts, mats and liners provide a soft transition from frame to picture and complement both.

As you read on you'll become aware of the subtleties of framing, matting and finishing. You should develop the confidence to enter a frame shop with art in hand and make a competent, artistic choice of both frame and insert materials. Best of all, you'll learn here how to make that frame and to finish it as well as cover your mat and cut the glass for your picture—all at minimal cost and, hopefully, at maximum pleasure.

Fig. 3. This striking picture with its simple frame turns this expanse of wall into a focal point of the room. The natural subject of the picture dictates a simple frame.

Fig. 4. A picture grouping arranged symmetrically over the sofa. Although aesthetically pleasing, it lacks the creative excitement of the asymmetrical grouping.

Fig. 5. Although asymmetrical, this picture arrangement gives a balanced impression. It provides a more interesting arrangement than a rigidly symmetrical one.

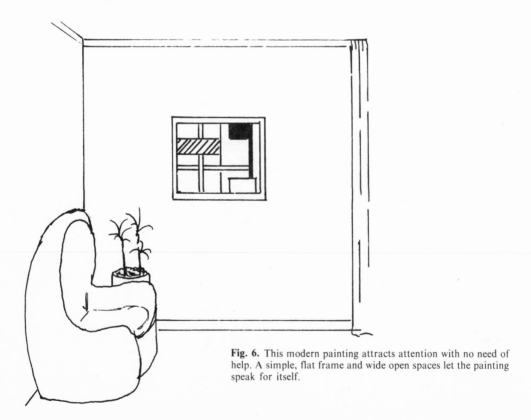

Fig. 6. This modern painting attracts attention with no need of help. A simple, flat frame and wide open spaces let the painting speak for itself.

Fig. 7. These family collections are divided into two groups: family portraits hang on one wall and family certificates and documents hang on another wall. The bottom pictures of both collections are hung at the same level.

8

Fig. 8. The wide mat on this picture helps provide a smooth transition from the stone wall to the print.

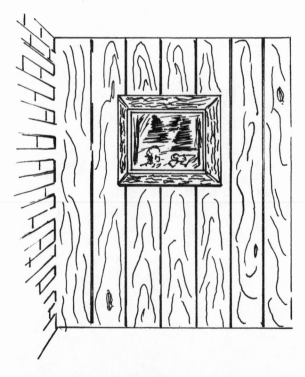

Fig. 9. The dark stain on this frame acts as a clear divider between the wall paneling and the picture. Note the white edge on the inside of the frame. It helps separate and bring out this somber-toned picture from its frame.

Chapter 2

Design Elements That Make the Completed Picture

Although the same picture can be framed in any number of ways and still be aesthetically pleasing in each way, some basic precepts can guide you in your framing project. Following these precepts will help assure you of achieving a total effect for your picture that will delight you. This chapter introduces basic guidelines, which will help in choosing framing materials at the professional framer or when doing your own framing.

First, have in mind where you intend to place the picture. As mentioned in the first chapter, a textured wall or paneling will make a difference in your choice of material, color and proportion.

A frame should be compatible with the picture it surrounds, neither upstaging it nor underdefining it. The frame should complement the picture in two ways: it should suit the *subject* of the picture and, along with its inserts, it should suit the *style* or treatment of the picture.

Frame Types

For the sake of discussion, let's classify frames into three very broad categories that would be compatible with various art subjects: traditional frames, provincial frames and modern/contemporary frames. Traditional frames are those elaborate ornamental frames that are antiqued or gold leafed. These are the dangerously enticing frames that are so often unsuited to the picture they contain. So many times a clean and simple piece of art is overwhelmed by a traditional frame. The frames *do* attract attention, which is probably the reason for the choice. All too often, though, such a frame dominates the art. The proper subject to be contained within these frames is of a classical nature such as found in the old masters.

Provincial frames are those with natural wood graining and natural color or a slight stain. Natural settings and still life pictures such as fruit, flowers, bottles or a combination of these are compatible in provincial frames. These frames are also well suited to landscapes and primitives.

The modern or contemporary frames are simple in design, finished in solid or textured colors or in metal. Modern art, graphics, boldly decorative compositions and geometrics are well matched with these frames.

In short, the subject of the picture is one element that dictates the choice of frame, either traditional, provincial or modern.

Fig. 10. Here's a small sample of the many picture frames that are commercially made. The frame shop where this picture was taken had another wall as large as this one—covered with still more frame styles.

Frame Traditions

The method or treatment used in a work of art should also be considered when choosing a frame. In addition, art method is taken into consideration when choosing the inserts—liners, mats and fillets. Tradition dictates that certain art treatments or mediums be framed in certain ways:

GRAPHICS and MAPS are usually framed in narrow wooden or metal frames. Mats are soft and often off-white. The important plate mark on a print should not be hidden by the mat. Also the edges of the map or graphic are sometimes part of the work and should not be hidden. Glass or plastic is used for protection.

GOUACHES are similar to watercolors, but are stronger and more opaque, and therefore can have a heavier frame than is used for watercolors. Usually glass and mat are also used in framing gouaches.

OIL PAINTINGS are not matted or covered with glass. Sometimes a liner may be used. The frame must be strong so as to keep the wooden stretcher from warping.

PASTELS usually require shallow and narrow frames, with a liner to keep the glass from touching the chalky surface.

PHOTOGRAPHS are best framed in a narrow frame, but can also be effective when simply mounted with or without borders on a block of wood or on plastic foam. When framed, mats and glass are used. The photo print is almost always rubber cemented or heat sealed to a mounted board to keep it flat.

REPRODUCTIONS of oil paintings are usually treated in the same style as the original. Color, texture and size determine whether the surfaces of other types of reproductions need glass protection.

WATERCOLORS usually are framed in shallow, narrow frames with medium to wide mats.

Fig. 11. This picture of waving palms and tumultuous ocean is of a dynamic nature that works well with its ornate, gilded frame in the traditional style. (JULIUS LOWY)

Fig. 12. A stylized version of cornflowers combines with a simple, provincial frame of pine laminate for a natural, fresh effect. (GREG COPELAND, INC.)

Fig. 13. A mirror graphic, taken from a pinball machine, is framed in a sleek silver metal frame. (ALUMINUM SECTION FRAME, INC.)

Fig. 14. The no-white-frame rule has its exceptions, as shown by this delicate pen and ink drawing with watercolor, "Takayama Japan." Note that the art floats in the narrow, white metal frame and gently textured mat. (BY BETTY GUY)

Fig. 15. Frame and liner are both silvered antique, separated by a white linen mat. Watercolor is "Brooklyn Winter." (BY BETTY GUY)

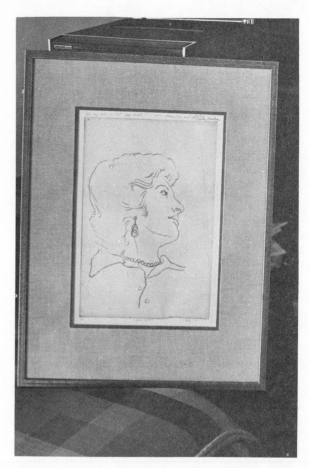

Fig. 16. A painting can take on a monumental feeling with help from its frame. This miniature, "Paris Rain," is only three by five and one-half inches and is in a black and gold frame. (BY BETTY GUY)

Fig. 17. The narrow brown liner serves to bring out the sepia tone of this etching of poet Shirley Kaufman Dileski. The heavy linen mat is a good choice for transition between frame and liner. (BY BETTY GUY)

Experiment with corner samples of different frames to see what their effect is on your art. In general, you'll find that elaborate frames are not suitable for photos, watercolors, pastels or graphics, especially when the subject is natural or delicate. A white frame is rarely suitable, since light color doesn't help focus in on the picture. A darker frame will make the white in the picture pop out.

Inserts

After the frame is chosen we then select the inserts: the liners, mats and fillets. A "liner" is a wooden frame molding from 3/8 inch to over six inches wide, usually covered with linen, metal leaf or lacquer. It is a transitional element between the painting and frame. A "mat" is a sheet, usually made of cardboard, laid over a picture with a window cut out for showing the picture. The mat protects the art from direct contact with glass, serves a decorative function and focuses attention on the subject. A "fillet" is a second mat under the first mat. It is of a contrasting color or in metal leaf. Its sole purpose is decorative. Besides providing a visual separation

Fig. 18. This miniature of Galway Bay, Ireland, with its dark color values has a striking effect when combined with a dark narrow liner and a light wide mat. (BY BETTY GUY)

from the frame and transition to the art, the mat separates the art and the glass that protects it from smoke, grease, light, heat and soot.

It is an optical illusion that we perceive the middle of a vertical line to be higher than it actually is. To counter this illusion, the bottom of the mat should actually be cut wider than the top, so that we perceive the picture as being in the middle.

Often *stitchery* that is to be framed is not square. The mat opening must be cut out of square, too . . . or several out of square fillets can be built up until you can cut a square mat that is compatible.

Mats and liners serve the same aesthetic purpose—a smooth transition from frame to subject. They are used on different types of subjects as mentioned previously, and for different functional reasons. Generally a mat can be two and one half inches wide at top and sides and three inches at the bottom. Widths are larger for larger pictures. The first liner is usually 3/8 to 1/2 inch wide, of gold, silver, colored lacquer or fabric covered.

Proportions

Neither a liner nor a mat should be of the same width as the frame or any of the frame's detail panels. This avoids monotony and the need for your eyes to stop after traveling the same distance twice, therefore reacting to the frame rather than the picture. The mistake is usually avoided with a mat because a picture requiring one is most often surrounded by a frame that is narrower than the mat.

At times, in place of a liner, you might want to use a frame that has an inside panel of gold, silver or colored lacquer. This provides a transition from frame to picture without the use of a liner.

A fillet or second mat under the first mat creates a pleasing effect. It is especially recommended on subjects that serve a totally decorative purpose, photographs, etchings and serigraphs. For example, a decorative love poem might be done on parchment, printed in black, with some red and gold illumination. A red fillet can be topped by a gold fillet, topped by a mat of parchment color and then surrounded by a black or red frame. Double fillets can be used to play against each other and to bring out colors in the picture. They can also be used under a neutral mat, as in this example.

Colors

When choosing color and material for frame and inserts, keep in mind that they should blend with the subject. The mat should blend with the picture; as mentioned, it is not good to use a mat to go with colors in the room.

The mat color is often suggested by the picture. You might want to choose a mat from the color that is in the picture to the smallest degree. The mat is often a subtle color. Bright colors can be saved for the fillet. The exception is with purely decorative or whimsical pictures which often sparkle with a bright mat.

Too often, particularly with photographs, the framing choice is not really planned and the subject is not taken into consideration. The easy standard choice is a black frame with a white mat. If you frame photographs you might consider a dark wood frame and an off-white or ivory mat. They would lend the same impression without giving the stark effect of black and white.

Materials

Burlap appears to be a favorite material for covering mats. Despite its widespread use, burlap is often difficult to handle. Its wide weave allows glue to seep through to the top of the mat and makes fitting corners difficult. In addition, some professionals dislike using burlap because it contains active chemicals. The fabric alternatives are many, ranging from linen to delicate silks, satins and velvets.

Generally, heavy textures are chosen for "rugged" subjects and fine textures are chosen for "subtle" delicate subjects. Silks and satins should be chosen with care because they often have a sheen that may or may not be compatible with the subject.

Velvets are rather difficult to work with, because their pile can become crushed in the corners. It can also separate along the mat edges if pulled too tightly.

If you want to use a certain specific texture, material or frame in a particular room, a mirror can accommodate a framing preference more easily than can a work of art.

Chapter 3

Framing Your Art the Easiest Way

After considering the design elements involved in picture framing, you may decide that you'd like to be gently initiated into the craft. Instead of tackling a framing project from the very beginning of cutting and joining the frame, and working through to the very end of putting a finish on the frame, you can choose alternatives that lighten your work load. There are a surprising number of alternates entailing varying degrees of work between taking your art to a professional framer and having him frame your picture and doing the entire project yourself. You may decide (1) to go to a frame-it-yourself shop and frame your picture, (2) to purchase a frame kit and assemble it, or (3) to purchase a ready-made frame and merely insert your picture.

Visiting a Frame-It-Yourself Shop

Frame-it-yourself shops have all the equipment and materials you need to frame your picture. You simply bring your art and make your own frame. The shops are widespread in the Midwest, coming into their own on the West Coast. They are beginning to sprout in the East, too. The charge for framing your art, depends on the frame type, number of mats and type of glass. But it is usually much less than going to a custom frame shop and somewhat more than doing it in your home.

In an afternoon or evening you can frame a number of pictures and hang them in your abode that same night. It's also a good way to learn the basics of framing before you begin to make your own frames completely.

In a frame shop, however, the frame selection is not as large as you could create using combined builders' moldings. Plus, you miss the fun of experimenting and putting a finish on your frame. If both time and money are considerations, a frame-it-yourself shop may be the best place for you to begin your framing experience.

Take your art to the shop. Similar to a custom frame shop, the frame-it-yourself shop has a display of mats and frames from which you can make your selection. You choose a frame, glass and mat based on your particular design considerations. A clerk will cut the materials to the correct size and give you the needed tools and supplies.

You might then be stationed in front of a vise at a long work table. The table will have vises every three or four feet for other customers. Since the materials are already cut, your helper will give you instructions on how to glue and nail the frame together, then how to assemble the frame components for your finished picture.

You'll be left to work as slow or as fast as you wish, although your helper might check to see if you have questions. This way of learning to frame is quite enjoyable, especially when the result can be that you have your finished piece tucked under an arm and are on the way home to hang it. One added advantage—any questions that occur to you can be answered by the store helper.

Brackets, Corner Frames and Frame Kits

A faster and easier way of framing your art than making a frame is by using brackets, corner frames or a framing kit. All are available in hobby shops, art supply stores and often business supply and hardware stores.

The brackets and corner frames are a rather temporary way of framing art—especially good if you want to change the art occasionally. Both are available in metal, black and white enamel and clear acrylic. There are two brackets to a set; one fits the top center of your art, and the other fits on the bottom center. They clamp the art and framing components together. The four corner clamps operate much like the brackets except for their positioning.

You may want to add glass or acrylic, a mat, a mount and backing to the art or you may want to keep it much simpler. However, the art will need either a mount or a backing to keep it rigid. These methods of framing are especially good for photographs, graphics and modern art.

Framing sections are only slightly more involved to assemble. They are available in metal and several colors. The frame is purchased in two packs, each containing two sides of the frame. One pair of sides is the same measurement as the depth of your art. The other pair of sides is the same measurement as the width of your art. The hardware needed to make the frame is included.

Since framing sections make a more permanent frame than brackets, you will probably want to add glass, backing and a mat to the art (kits containing a mounting board, acrylic cover and backing are also available). This frame can be made in a matter of minutes. With a minimum effort you can hang your art in brackets, corner frames or a section frame.

Ready-Made Frames

The fastest and easiest way of framing your art is to select a ready-made frame. This may be necessary when time doesn't permit you to make a frame. Besides, there are more and more attractive ready-made frames on the market, in a wide selection of materials, ranging from acrylics to cork to burlap frames. If you have a standard size work of art or photograph to be framed, you should look at the frames produced commercially.

Acrylic Frames

At the mention of ready-made frames, the first frames to come into mind are the clear acrylic frames that can be easily used in many ways. They serve principally as a structure to encase and protect the picture and as a means to hang or stand the art.

Perhaps the most familiar of these frames is the DAX Frame, from Art Infinitum, Inc. It is a clear acrylic, borderless frame in which the art slips between the clear front and the component box. Although there is no frame edge to focus one's attention, the picture is projected from the wall due to the thickness of the component box.

Another acrylic frame, the Trap Frame by Kulicke Frames, Inc., gives the impression that the art is suspended in space in front of the wall. The wall then becomes the mat around the picture. The art is actually placed between two clear acrylic sheets, banded together at the top and bottom by narrow strips of polished aluminum. Hangers are attached to the back acrylic sheet to float the frame one-half inch away from the wall.

The WK Warhol Kulicke Frame is a free-standing, acrylic frame, for placing art on tables and shelves. It has both a clear front and a clear back and is ideal for displaying two works of art, or one work that has a front and a back side. It is also available with a colored acrylic back when only one side displays art. The frame is made with two acrylic sheets held together by narrow, clear plastic bands. It provides an inexpensive method of presenting small graphics, drawings, cards, photographs, prints or memorabilia.

Similar to the original DAX Frame, but with an opaque black or white border, the DAX Float Frame is aptly named because the art seems to be suspended and framed within the border. The illusion is created by a deep ridge running between the clear acrylic covering the picture and the colored border, that makes the picture look as if it is not connected to the border.

Metal Frames

Sleek, metal frames are a natural go together with modern art or photographs. These frames are definite complements to a room with contemporary furnishings.

The Gallery Frames by Burnes of Boston are especially suitable for framing portraits or family pictures. They are available in brushed gold finish with your choice of one to five oval or rectangular picture openings.

The Aluminum Total Frame by Kulicke is made from extruded raw aluminum with invisible welded corners. It has a highly polished face and satin-finished sides which blend well with simple art, sketches or drawings.

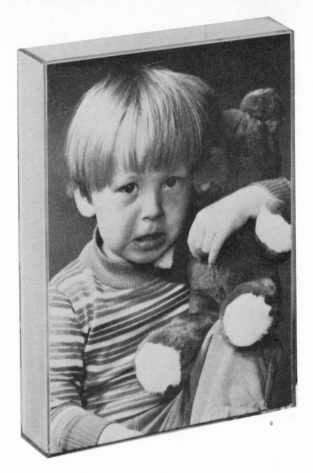

Fig. 19. DAX Frame

Fig. 20. Trap Frame

Fig. 21. WK Warhol Kulicke Frame

Fig. 22. DAX Float Frame

Fig. 23. Gallery Frame

Fig. 24. Aluminum Total Frame

Fig. 25. O Frame

Fig. 26. Daguerreotype Frame

Fig. 27. Grass Cloth Frame   **Fig. 28.** Cork Frame

Wood Frames

Although wood seems to dominate the scene in custom framing and do-it-yourself frame making, it takes a back seat to acrylic and metal frames in the ready-made variety. However, some very finely designed wood frames are now being produced on a ready-made basis.

The O Frame from Kulicke is a prime example of an attractive wood ready-made frame. It is crafted of natural, light wood with rounded corners connected by butterfly splines. No nails are used in the frame. This combination of material and design make the O Frame suitable for framing a variety of subjects both old and new.

Two Burnes of Boston wood frame designs are well chosen for framing portraits. Their romantic daguerreotype frame is wood with gold metal leaf and a filigreed mat of antique gold-toned metal. It is available with up to three oval openings. Burnes' straightforward approach to a wood frame has a narrow gold border around the picture opening. This frame is available with two or three picture openings, either oval or rectangular.

Novel Frame Materials

A frame of baked ceramic or one covered with cork involves steps that are not easily copied for mass production. Therefore, hand crafted frames are more readily made with novel materials than are ready-made ones. Burnes of Boston has produced several frames utilizing materials not often found in ready-mades. Their series of grass cloth frames includes frames with single and up to five rectangular picture openings. They also have cork frames with single rectangular openings. The glass cloth and cork serve as a mat edged in metal around the picture.

Fig. 29. Wood Frame with Mat

Chapter 4

Mounting the Art

For practical reasons prints, maps, photographs and drawings should be mounted or fastened to heavier backing. Mounts can be invisible and merely serve to give the subject more substance and permanence. Mounts can also have the aesthetic purpose of serving as a mat border.

Prints are usually reproduced on white paper. When they are mounted, the white border around them should not be visible. It should either be trimmed or covered by a fillet or mat.

Original graphics usually are not mounted. Collectors like the graphics to remain loose for easy handling when they are displayed for sale. However, if you're sure you'll want to keep your graphic, you might want to mount it for support.

Types of Mount Boards

Mount boards come in many weights and thicknesses to vary with the types of art to be mounted. The mounting material that is easiest to use is foam core board. It consists of styrofoam laminated between two sheets of white oaktag or brown kraft paper. The board is lightweight, rigid and very easy to cut.

Temlock and Upson board are also commonly used. Temlock is slightly porous and ideal for mounting maps, charts and bulletin boards that might take pins or thumbtacks. Upson board is heavier and more rigid than Temlock.

Illustration board and both regular and double-thick mat board are used for mounting. Art that demands a thick board to lend extra support can be mounted on masonite, plasterboard or chipboard.

The mount should keep the item being framed flat and free from warpage. Therefore, the larger or heavier the item, the thicker the mount board should be. A thin board backing a large item will tend to warp because of changes in the humidity.

If you don't plan to mat the object being framed and intend the mount to be the background, you may want to choose white foam core board or a colored mat board. Or you might mount the art on decorative paper and in turn adhere that paper to a basic mount—this is called "countermounting." With this technique you can devise countless mountings for your art—all types of fabrics, decorative papers and cork, to name only a few.

After the type of mount board has been selected the kind of adhesive is decided upon. It should have good holding power and not create excess warpage when it dries. The type of adhesive to be used will depend in part on the type of mount process used. When mounting art it is so important to keep your hands and tools clean. It's much better to take it slowly and not get glue on the face of the art than to be bothered with having to remove it, even if removing is possible.

Art Positioning

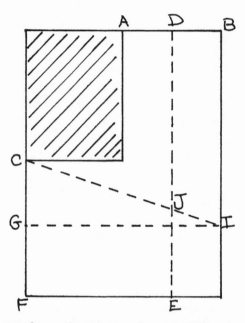

Before going into the various mounting processes, here's a foolproof way to properly position your art that will land it in the right place every time:

1. Place the art in the upper left hand corner of your mounting board. The art's top right and lower left corners A and C respectively.

2. Divide the remaining space AB in half to find point D.
3. Draw a very light pencil line DE.
4. Repeat with CF to find G and draw GI.
5. Draw a diagonal from point C to point I.
6. Line CI intersects DF at point J, which is the final position for the lower right hand corner of your art.
7. Align the right edge of the art with DE and erase the line.

MOUNTING PROCESSES

There are three mounting techniques: adhesive mounting, dry mounting and wet mounting. We will take a close look at adhesive mounting and dry mounting. Wet mounting is used primarily for damaged or folded subjects. It's a complicated process that involves forcing the paper to stretch then allowing it to shrink.

Adhesive Mounting

Adhesive Mounting is the least complicated process from the standpoint that it requires no special equipment. The subject is simply glued to the mount. This can be done by either glue or spray adhesive or by using sheets of double-stick film.

To use glue or spray adhesive, first decide if you want the mount to show; if so, position the art on the mount as suggested. If you don't want the mount to show, simply measure the print carefully to check for squareness, then mark off its size on the mount board. With a mat knife cut the board to size. Use either a white glue or spray rubber cement such as 3M's Spra-ment Adhesive. If you use the white glue, brush it on the mounting board covering the surface. Then even it out being sure that you use only enough to entirely cover the board. Otherwise, the glue will seep out the sides of the print and might get on it while you're smoothing it out.

If you use spray adhesive, spray the mount surface evenly and let it dry until tacky. Then firmly press down on your art, pressing out bubbles. Begin in its center and flatten it outward toward the edges. You may want to place a paper over the print to prevent getting glue on it. Clamp the mounted art between two pieces of plywood, or place glass over it and stack books on it to weigh it down.

Adhesive film is also practical for adhering the print to the board. The film is papered on both sides by waxed paper. First, cut the papered film to the size of the print. Then peel the waxed paper off one side and carefully press it onto the mounting board where the print is to be placed. Next peel the paper off the other side of the film and very carefully press down your art—exactly as you want it. The adhesives are quite strong and don't permit you to shift the subject once it is down.

Dry Mounting

In the dry-mounting process a special paper called "mounting tissue" is used. This paper has been coated with a plastic adhesive that becomes sticky when heat and pressure are applied.

To dry mount your art simply cut the mounting tissue to the size of the subject. After positioning it, attach it to the mounting board in several places with your clothes iron (a professional tacking iron is used by photographers and framers). Place the subject over the tissue and mounting board and thoroughly heat and bond all together as you apply pressure with your iron—or all are placed in a dry-mounting press to bond. The dry-mount process is used on small prints and photographs primarily.

A word of caution when you dry mount photographs, especially color pictures where the emulsion is softer: you might want to use your iron at small intervals rather than one continuous ironing so as not to damage the emulsion. This procedure will assure a bonding of the art to the mount board.

Handy Hints

1. If you plan to use a print that has been rolled for a long period of time or has been mailed to you in a tube, you may want to flatten it before trying to mount it. It can be flattened so as to be handled with ease if you roll it in the reverse way on a length of paper, tape it and leave it that way for several days.

2. At times you may want to remove art from a mount that has been temporarily mounted with dabs of rubber cement (heaven forbid). Your chances of success will be greater if you place the art face down and try to remove the backing by rolling it or peeling it away from the art.

3. Scotch tape that has been carelessly stuck on the art can possibly be removed by carefully applying methyl ethyl ketone (also called butanone) a little at a time until the scotch tape comes off. The tape may leave some discoloration, however.

Fig. 30. Materials needed for mounting your art are: metal straightedge, glue, brush, pencil, X-acto knife, mount board and clean rag. Foam core board and white glue are used in this example. The art is a reproduction of Picasso's "The Three Musicians," measuring 21½ by 23¼ inches. It will be framed as we proceed.

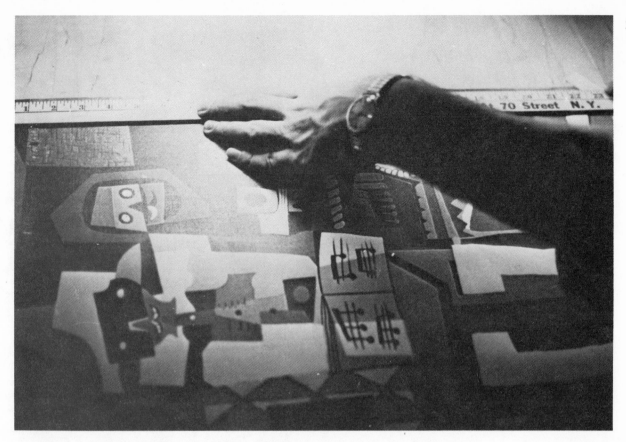

Fig. 31. Mark off the dimensions of the art as it is placed over the mount board. However, if you want the mount to show, position the art as suggested earlier on the mount; then mark off the dimensions you want the mount to be.

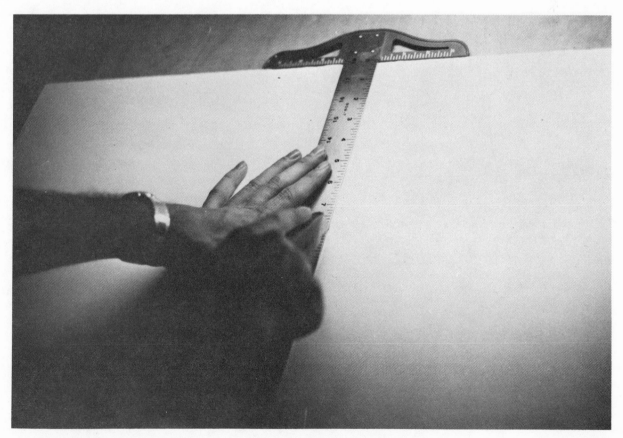

Fig. 32 Cut the mount board with an X-acto knife, using metal straightedge as a guide.

Fig. 33. Apply an even, very thin coat of glue over the entire area of the mount board that the art will cover. If too much glue is used it will seep out the sides of the print. If too little is used, the art will not adhere in spots.

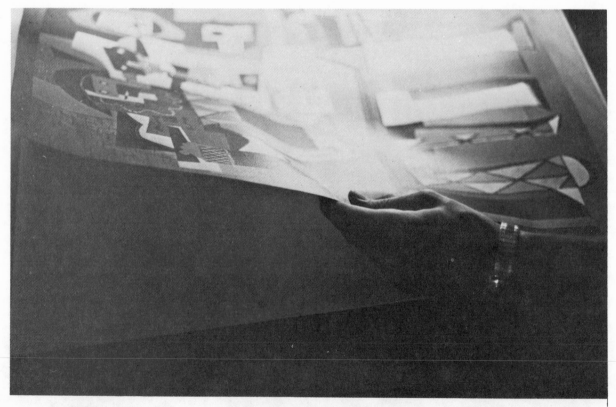

Fig. 34. Position your art on the mount board. Be sure the corners are even on the first side you place, because once your art is positioned it can only be repositioned with difficulty. Work quickly.

Fig. 35. Smooth the art down, beginning from the middle and working toward the edges. You can do this with a soft, clean rag—or you might want to invest in a roller. Be sure that glue does not seep from the edges and get on your art. You might want to cover it with a clean piece of paper before you begin smoothing to prevent glue seeping on the top side. You may want to weight the art while it is drying by placing books on it or by clamping it between two sheets of plywood or glass.

Chapter 5

Matting

A mat adds an extra decorative touch to a picture and provides a smooth transition from the picture frame to the picture. Considering the countless types of matboard to choose from, a mat can serve these aesthetic purposes handsomely for any art. Its utilitarian function is to protect the art from the glass. Mats serve both aesthetic and utilitarian purposes admirably if they are cut correctly. A properly cut mat has a deeper bottom than sides and top to accommodate our optical illusion that the center of a picture is higher than it actually is.

Specifically, the bottom depth of a mat should be a half inch or more than the sides and top. From experience it seems that the sides and top should never be less than two and one half inches in width. The maximum dimension can be far greater. For example, a striking enamel or a brilliantly colored miniature can carry a mat much wider than the actual work. However, the bottom depth is always wider than the top and side widths.

A mat less than two and one half inches wide will sometimes appear "skimpy" and certainly will not provide a smooth transition from the frame to the picture. An exception to this is a picture that is very narrow and tall, like the three ladies in Chapter 1. A mat with slender sides would then blend better with the picture emphasizing the picture's shape . . . which is the mat's function. The guidelines are here, but it's up to your aesthetic discretion to make a proper mat choice.

When choosing mat color the same factors must be as when choosing a frame . . . namely subject type and style. That vibrant enamel might be dazzling with a mat of strong color, either similar or contrasting. On the other hand, a delicate watercolor of a field of flowers would be destroyed with a bright mat.

Types of Mats

There is a tremendous wealth of colors and textures found in matboards. Besides the regular board there are metallic finishes. Boards are also available with a different color on each side to give two color choices. The textures produced are also varied—linen, burlap and silk matboards are being manufactured.

You might choose to make your mat from plexiglass or glass sprayed with color. Or if you simply can't find the right mat, you can cover your own or add a special texture to a mat. Both alternatives open a vast number of possibilities for creating individualized mats.

How to Cut the Mat

Mats are cut from the back. Begin by placing the matboard face down. Decide on the overall size of the mat by placing the art on it. Then mark off the outer dimensions with your yardstick as a guide. Cut the matboard to the measured size. Placing the art on the board again, decide this time how large you want the mat opening and mark it. (Be sure that the edges of the art will not be visible when the mat window is cut.) Set a compass to the dimensions you've marked and with the metal point held against the side of the mat draw the compass along the top and

Fig. 36. This mat is being cut with a mat cutter. To get a perfectly beveled edge merely glide the cutter along the metal straightedge.

sides. Reset the compass for the wider bottom and mark it off in the previous manner.

Your X-acto mat knife must be very sharp when cutting. It is good to sharpen it with a whetstone before each cut. With a straightedge held along the markings, push the knife into the matboard at the proper angle that you want for the bevel. Start about one-eighth inch beyond the corner marking. Cut the first side in one even stroke ending about one-eighth inch beyond the marking. The remaining three sides are cut in the same manner. Then the center should be completely disengaged. If you do make a slightly rough cut, the edge can be smoothed with sandpaper.

Turn the mat right side up and place the art under it into the right position. Use a bit of masking tape at the top and bottom to keep the art in place. Again turning the art and matboard face down tape the four sides with masking tape; or for more permanence use gummed brown paper tape.

Another way of attaching the mat to the mounting picture is with a tape "hinge." Place the top of the mounted picture and the top of the mat (face down) together so that they can be joined with one piece of tape. Place the tape half on the mount board and half on the matboard and then press. The mat is now adhered with a tape hinge.

Fig. 37. (Top) Materials needed for mat cutting are: matboard, straightedge, yardstick, mat knife, pencil, and compass.

Fig. 38. (Center) Measure the outer dimensions of your mat and mark them off on the back side of the mat.

Fig. 39. (Bottom) Cut the mat to its proper outer dimensions.

Fig. 40. (Top) Set your compass to the width you want the sides and top of your mat to be. Be sure that the edge of your art will not be visible when the window is cut—unless the edges are part of the art.

Fig. 41. (Center) Mark off the dimensions of the sides and top of the mat with your compass. The metal point of the compass should glide along the outer edge of the mat and act as a guide. Reset the compass somewhat wider for the bottom mat measurement, and mark it.

Fig. 42. (Bottom) Cut the mat by placing your knife about ⅛-inch beyond a corner and bringing it down in one smooth stroke at a bevel angle. The overcut of ⅛-inch insures that the corners will be sharp. The overcut will not be noticeable on the face of the mat.

Fig. 43. (Top) Sand any rough spots on the bevel edges. They can often be smoothed.

Fig. 44. (Center) Position the art in the mat and tape it. This can be done most easily by working on the edge of the table.

Fig. 45. (Bottom) Secure the art with masking tape on all four sides. For permanence you may want to use gummed brown paper tape or strips of rice paper and nonacidic school paste.

Fig. 46. (Top) Hinge the mounted art and mat together by placing the top of the mounted picture and the top of the mat (face down) together and joining them with masking tape.

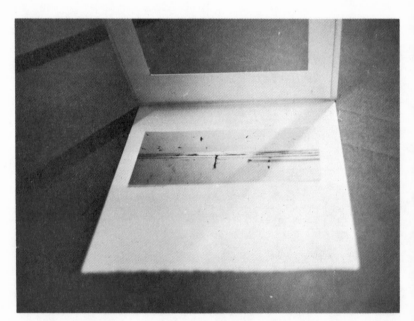

Fig. 47. (Center) Flop the mat over the art and your job is finished.

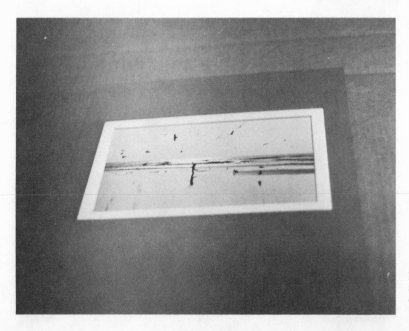

Fig. 48. (Bottom) These combined mats attract one's attention and direct it toward the picture, the overall tone of which is between the tone values of the mats. "Dancing Beach Girl" is by Roger Van Weelden.

Fig. 49. Another way of combining mats was demonstrated to us by Larry Taylor, owner of Aluminum Section Frames, Inc., New York City. Equal portions of two mats in contrasting colors are cut and exchanged. Masking tape is used to hold the insets in place.

Combining Mats

Mats can also be combined to bring out various colors or color shades in a picture. Fillets serve a purely decorative function. These "under mats" can go a long way in focusing one's eyes on a subject. The fillets have a slightly smaller opening than does the mat itself, which is on top. Fillets are cut with a *reverse bevel* so that the white within the board doesn't show. The fillets and top mat are attached together with white glue. Various kinds of glues are available, such as Elmer's Glue-All and Sobo Glue.

Covering and Finishing Mats

After looking through all of your art store's catalogs and considering glass, plastic and other materials, and you still can't find a suitable mat for your art, you might think about covering with fabric, or putting a textured finish on a mat. But, do keep in mind that the mat is supposed to blend with the picture. Restrain yourself from choosing a fabric that will steal admiration from the art.

Tools and materials you need for covering a mat are a scissors, X-acto knife, brush, fabric and white glue.

First be sure that the fabric you choose is heavy enough that your board does not show through it . . . or choose a board of the same color as the fabric. Cut the window in the board to the proper size. Cut the fabric to a size, about one inch larger on all sides than the mat. Using the brush apply a very thin, even coat of glue to the face of the mat. Spread the fabric flat and place the mat glue side down. Press lightly in place. Turning the mat and fabric face side up, lightly press and smooth the entire surface, being sure not to press so as to cause glue to seep through the cloth.

Cut each corner of the cloth at a 45-degree angle so that it doesn't overlap and bulge when folded. Again place the mat face down. Coat the entire outside edge of the mat back. Fold and smooth the outside edges of the fabric over the mat and press firmly. Leaving a one inch inside border, cut the window out of the mat. Starting about one eighth inch in from each inside mat corner, make a miter cut (a 45-degree-angle cut) in each corner on the material. Coat the entire inside edge of the mat with glue. Smooth the inside material over and onto the mat.

You might prefer to add a finish to a mat such as gold or copper leaf or a borghese finish (a silver leaf washed with raw sienna in a japan varnish). You might also try your own method of antiquing or stippling the mat with speckles. The methods for creating an individualized piece are numerous.

Glass mats are made by spraying several coats of enamel on the back of a piece of glass cut to mat size, then scribing the mat opening and lifting out the window piece. Since one of the functions of a mat is to separate the picture from the glass, you may want to add a fillet between your glass mat and your picture.

You might also consider gold leafing your glass mat. This can be done in much the same way that sign painters gold leaf a door or window. Dissolve a gelatin capsule in a pint of warm water and apply it with a brush to the glass mat. Squares of gold leaf can be purchased at an art store (and are fairly expensive). Score the gold leaf with your fingernail, separating it into about three smaller pieces. With a

Fig. 50. (Above) Materials needed to cover your mat are: fabric, mat, scissors, X-acto knife, white glue and brush.

Fig. 51. (Right) Cut the material about one inch larger than the mat on all sides.

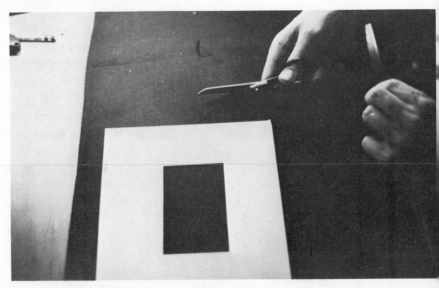

gilding brush, lift a portion of the leaf and place it on the glass mat, where it will readily be accepted by the gelatin preparation. Overlap the sections of leaf. When the mat is covered go over it with absorbent cotton to remove excess leaf and to burnish the leaf. When it is dry, stabilize the leaf with French varnish. Later go over it with varnish mixed with yellow pigment. Photos of gold leaf applied to a frame are shown in Chapter 7.

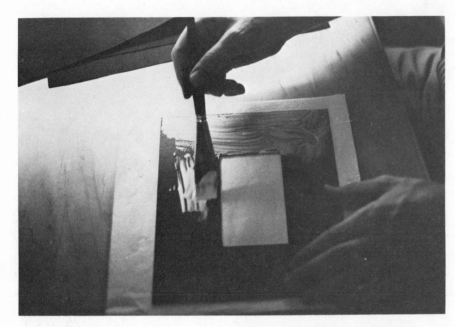

Fig. 52. (Left) Brush a very thin, even coat of glue over the face of the mat. We are using a black mat covered with black linen.

Fig. 53. (Below) Place the mat, glue side down, on the fabric and press lightly.

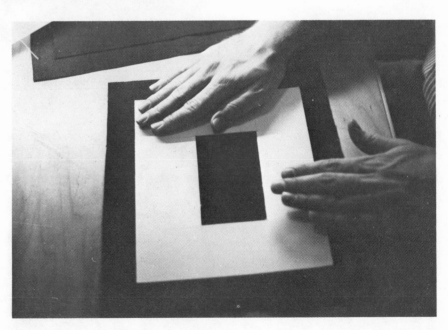

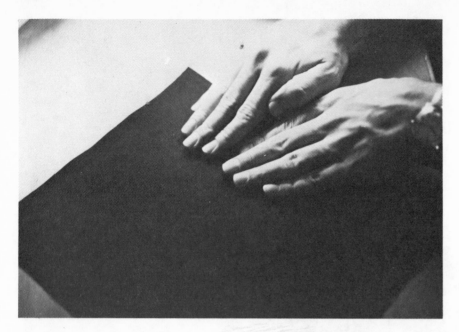

Fig. 54. (Top) Turn the mat face side up and lightly smooth the fabric, making certain that it is entirely glued to the mat board. Press lightly so that the glue won't seep through the fabric.

Fig. 55. (Center) Remove the corners of the fabric by cutting each off at a 45-degree angle. This will insure a smooth corner when the fabric is folded back and glued.

Fig. 56. (Bottom) Apply glue to the outside edge of the back of the mat.

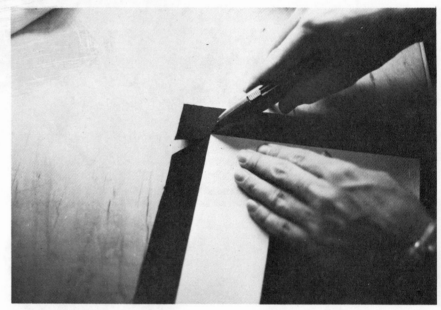

Fig. 57. (Top) Fold the outer edge of the fabric back on the glue.

Fig. 58. (Center) Cut out the window of the fabric, leaving about an inch to fold back.

Fig. 59. (Bottom) Make a miter cut about one-eighth inch in from each corner to allow for the thickness of the fabric. Apply glue to the matboard on the inside edge. Fold the fabric back on the glue.

Fig. 60. This acrylic "enamel" is in vibrant shades of blues and black. It is nicely set off by the white mount and wide black linen mat.

Fig. 61. Cut four strips of the fabric about two inches longer than the sides they will cover, and wide enough to cover the face of the liner and the rabbet.

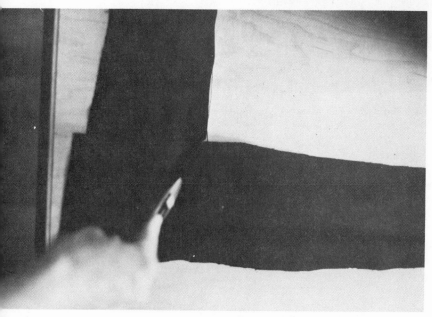

Fig. 62. (Top) Glue the strips to the face of the liner—they will overlap. Press the fabric lightly so the glue will not seep through it.

Fig. 63. (Center) Make a miter cut starting on the inside of each corner through both thicknesses of fabric.

Fig. 64. (Bottom) Lift the top piece of cloth and remove the excess bottom piece. Press the top piece back into position. If both pieces of fabric were cut together in the previous step, you should have a perfect match. Repeat for remaining corners.

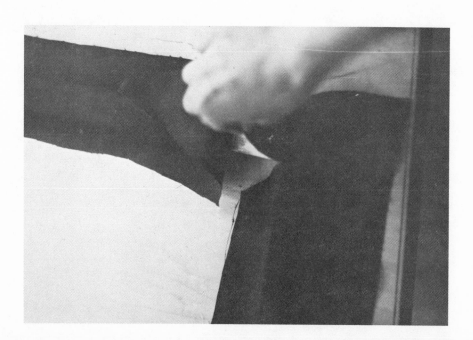

48

Fig. 65. Spread glue on the entire inside of the liner up to the rabbet. Fold the fabric over. Trim the fabric along the inside edge of the rabbet, as shown. Since the frame will hold the liner it isn't necessary to cover its outside edge. You can trim the excess fabric flush with the liner top.

Fig. 66. This covered insert will be used on "The Three Musicians" that is hung in Chapter 9.

Covering Liners

Liners are wooden frame inserts, next to the outside frame. They are usually covered with fabric or metal leaf. Liners are often used in place of a mat, particularly with paintings on canvas. Covering a liner is similar to covering a mat. Begin by cutting four strips of linen about two inches longer than the liner sides and wide enough to cover both the face and the entire *rabbet*. A rabbet is the extension of the back of the frame where the glass, mats and picture rest——more about this in the next chapter on constructing frames. Brush an even coat of glue over the face of one side of the insert. The strip overlaps the corners and edges. Do the same to the remaining sides. Press the cloth into the glue very gently. With an X-acto mat knife, start at the inside of one of the liner corners and very carefully miter cut (a 45-degree-angle cut) through both thicknesses of cloth where they overlap. Lift the top piece of fabric and remove the excess. Press the top piece of fabric back into position in the partially dried glue. Repeat this for the remaining three corners. Next, spread glue along the entire rabbet and fold the fabric around the inside edge. Trim the excess cloth off with your knife. Since the frame will hold the liner it is not necessary to cover its outside edge. Trim the excess material so the fabric edge is flush with the outside edge of the liner.

Corian: The Novelty Matting

Corian is a material that looks and feels like marble. It can be used as a mat to give a classic appearance to photographs and prints. Corian is a filled polymer developed by the Du Pont de Nemours Company. You can probably get remnants of the material at bath and kitchen shops. Larger sheets for bas reliefs and other art forms are available at building and plumbing suppliers. Corian is available in dawn beige, olive mist and cameo white colors in one-quarter, one-half and three-quarter-inch thicknesses.

To make a mat of this material use any standard wood-working tool to cut a one-half-inch thick piece of Corian to the inside dimensions of your picture frame. The frame should have a three-quarter-inch recess or rabbet to fit the Corian, glass, picture and backing. Shape the opening of the Corian with a router. The beauty of the material is that you can wet sand the scratches out after you rout. This is impossible to do with many other plastics—where scratches are permanent. Finish by rubbing the Corian with car polishing compound.

Handy Hint

If at some point a grease spot gets on one of your picture mats, it can be removed by taking the mat out of the frame and touching the spot with a bit of benzine (ligroine). Then place the mat in a bright spot of sunlight for a few minutes. Although you may have to repeat the process, the spot should eventually disappear without a trace.

Chapter 6

Making Picture Frames

We have already covered design considerations of framing art in Chapter 2. From that discussion you may have decided upon the type of frame, mat, etc., that you want to use. Now it's time to begin collecting material and equipment for the actual frame making—and then to begin making your frame.

Molding

Two main types of molding are used to frame pictures: regular picture molding and builder's molding, used in house trimming. The regular picture molding can be obtained at frame stores and the builder's molding is available at lumber supply stores. The difference between the two is that regular picture moldings have rabbets—an extension of the back where the glass, mats, picture and backing rest. The rabbet must be added to builder's moldings.

As the picture of the frame samples in Chapter 2 showed, there are many, many varieties of regular picture frame moldings. Also different types of builder's moldings can be used by themselves or in combinations to form other designs. Frame finishes and mat choices further broaden the creative element in framing a picture, and assure the framer that with a little ingenuity he or she can arrive at countless "original framing combinations."

TOOLS YOU'LL NEED

Following are the principal tools needed for constructing a frame: miter box and backsaw, framing clamp, C-clamps, hammer, brads, rulers and glue. Other helpful tools will be mentioned as we go along.

Miter Box and Backsaw

Perhaps the most important equipment to the framer are his miter box and backsaw. With proper usage and alignment they can assure the framer of getting the exact 45-degree mitered angles necessary in frame making.

The range of miter boxes begins with a very basic wood miter box which costs a few dollars and continues with miter boxes at intermediate levels up to those costing several hundred dollars. Initially inexpensive miter boxes make good frames.

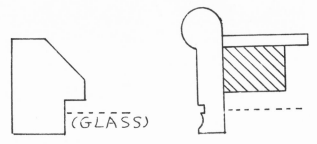

Fig. 67. Regular picture molding like that on the left already has a rabbet to accommodate the glass, mat, picture and backing. A rabbet has been added (shaded area) to the combination builder's molding on the right. The rabbet is a standard ½ by ¾-inch parting strip.

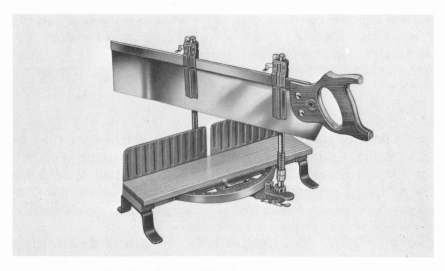

Fig. 68. (Above) 60 MB Miter Box and Backsaw

Fig. 69. (Below) No. 115 Miter Box.

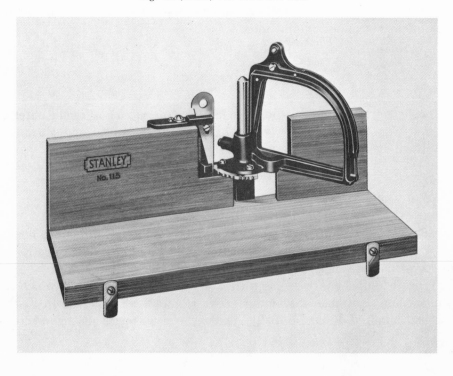

Fig. 70. (Above) These are a few samples of the different varieties of builder's molding available. Two or more can be used in combination to make a limitless number of different frame designs.

Fig. 71. (Below) Miter Clamps.

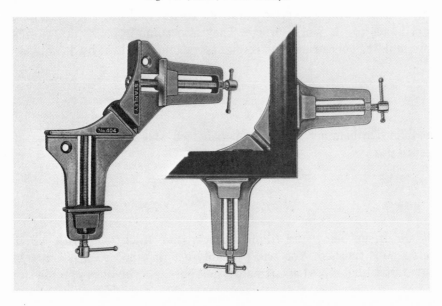

But over a period of time with use, they tend to wear and become wobbly. However, you might prefer beginning with an inexpensive miter box and purchase a more professional one as you progress—you will be well compensated by its fine performance.

A wood miter box was used to make the frame shown in the illustrations in this chapter. The mitered corners turned out nicely. However, it is suggested that if you plan to continue framing, get a moderately priced miter box such as the Stanley 60 MB, shown in the photo with the backsaw, or the Stanley 115.

It is necessary to use a backsaw for picture framing. Ordinary carpenter saws don't have reinforced backs and are too wobbly to insure a true 45-degree angle. As with miter boxes, backsaws are available in a broad price range, but one of intermediate price will probably be quite adequate.

Framing Clamps

The framing clamp holds two mitered ends of the adjacent sides of a frame together after they have been glued so that they can form a corner. It is important that the clamp hold the ends together properly so as to allow the glue to set and to keep the joints in position while nailing brads into it. Corner clamps and clamps designed for the express purpose of clamping mitered ends of a picture frame together are available. They are fairly inexpensive, so you may want to buy two of them so that two angles at a time can be glued.

A miter vise is an excellent alternative to the framing clamps, although it is more expensive. However, if you have a work shop, it might be to your advantage to purchase a vise, because it has uses in other projects.

C-Clamps

A few C-clamps would be good additions to the tool set. These can be used to clamp miter boxes to the work surface. They also come in handy in rare instances when frame molding—because of its roundness—cannot be held by a framing clamp.

Hammer

A medium-size hammer that is well balanced and rests comfortably in your hand is best to use.

Brads

Brads are driven below the frame surface, then filled over with wood putty before the frame is finished. You will probably use 3/4 inch to 1-1/2 inch brads in your work. Start with a mixed assortment, then purchase the ones you use the most.

Rulers

Since accuracy is the keyword in framing, the importance of accurate measuring instruments is stressed. An accurate yardstick would be very useful.

Glue

White glue is the easiest and most effective to use. Brand names include Sobo Glue and Elmer's Glue-All.

Making a Rabbet for Your Frame

When you use builder's molding you'll want to add a rabbet to it to secure the glass, mat, picture and backing. To make the rabbet you'll need a saw, framing clamp, hammer, yardstick, pencil, glue and 1-1/2 inch brads. Standard parting strips 1/2 by 3/4 inch can be used effectively to make a rabbet for builder's molding. The "rabbet frame" can be butt joined since it won't show. The corners needn't be mitered, but can be cut straight to form square-corner joints. Then the rabbet frame can be glued, and tacked to the back of the outside frame with 3/4 inch brads. Making the rabbet will be a good warm-up for making the liner or frame.

Remember, accuracy in measurement is very important. The rabbet size should be about 1/8 inch wider and deeper than the size of the picture, just to be sure that the glass, mat, picture and backing will fit comfortably. Also remember that the butt ends will overlap 3/4 inch on top and bottom, so add an extra 1-1/2 inches to the long pieces. For example, if the picture is 8 by 10 inches, two parting strips should be cut 8-1/8 inches and two parting strips should be cut 11-5/8 inches (10 inches, plus 3/4 inches top overlap, plus 3/4 inches bottom overlap, plus 1/8 inch accommodation.

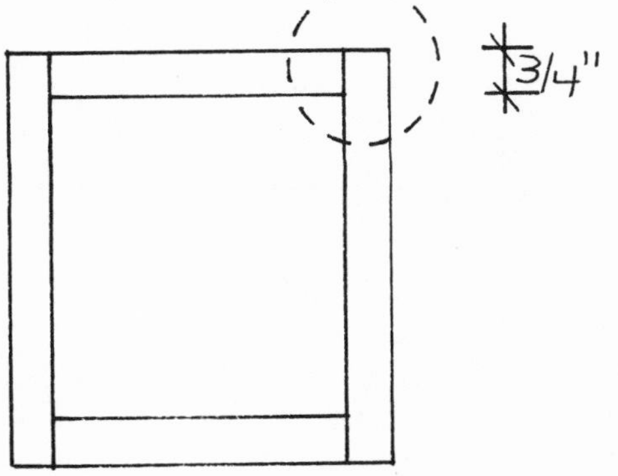

Fig. 72. The butt ends of the rabbet will overlap ¾-inch on the top and ¾-inch on the bottom. After you have measured the art add an extra 1½ inches for the overlaps and ⅛ inch extra accommodation room to the measurement of the long sides of your frame.

Mark off, then cut the first short side of your rabbet. Use the first short side to measure off the second short side then cut it. Do the same with the two long sides. At this point you might check to see that the size is correct by placing the pieces around your art.

Glue a long and short side together. Be sure the long end overlaps the short side. Place the pieces in the framing clamp ready for nailing. Use 1-1/2 inch brads to nail the corner—two to a corner for a total of eight nails. The other long and short ends should be joined in the same manner. Then the two sections should be joined together for the complete rabbet.

The rabbet can be added to an outside frame as already mentioned, or it can be added to a liner (a frame within the major frame). In the following discussion we add the rabbet to the liner. It is added to the outer frame in exactly the same way.

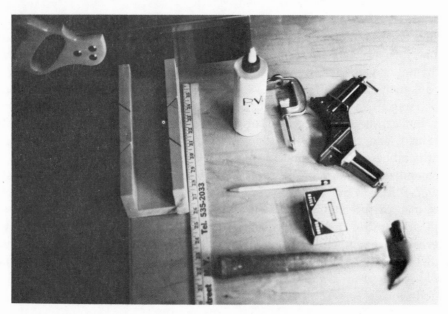

Fig. 73. Materials needed to make a rabbet are: saw, framing clamp, hammer, yardstick, pencil, glue and 1½ inch brads. In addition, you'll need ¾ by ½-inch parting strip—enough to encompass your picture, plus overlap. You may want to use a miter box to cut square corners.

Making a Liner for Your Frame

Paintings done on canvas and their reproductions aren't matted, or covered with glass and therefore usually rely on liners for a smooth transition from frame to art. Liners are simply inner frames. For detailed instructions on making them see "How to Make a Frame" below. Liners are constructed exactly like the outer frame, using the same principles as in making a rabbet. You'll need a miter box, backsaw, framing clamp, hammer, yardstick, pencil, strip of molded stop or clam molding (whatever is to be used for the insert), 3/4 inch and 1-1/4 inch brads and glue.

The allowance for mitered corners is different from that of butt-joined square-corner joints. You must allow twice the width of the frame molding. So, for

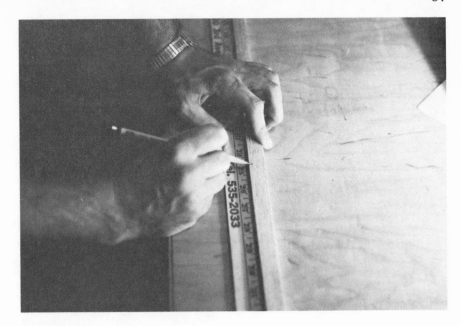

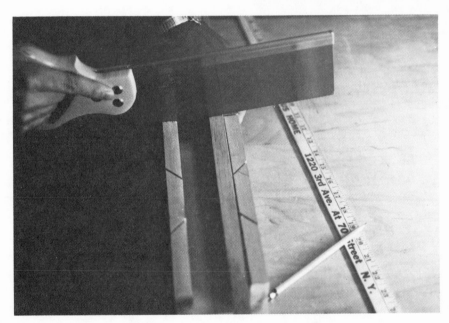

Fig. 74. (Top) Measure the first short side of your art and mark it off (allowing ⅛ inch for extra room) on the parting strip.

Fig. 75. (Center) Cut the first short side of your rabbet. Since the rabbet will not show it is not necessary to miter the ends. A butt joint (square-corner joint) will be stronger. (If you use a wood miter box, place a cutting block under the parting strip to elevate it.)

Fig. 76. (Bottom) Mark the length of the other short side, using the first as a guide. This will insure that both pieces are the same length. Cut the second short side. Do the same to the long sides—be sure to allow ¾-inch each for top and bottom overlap and extra ⅛-inch for room.

58

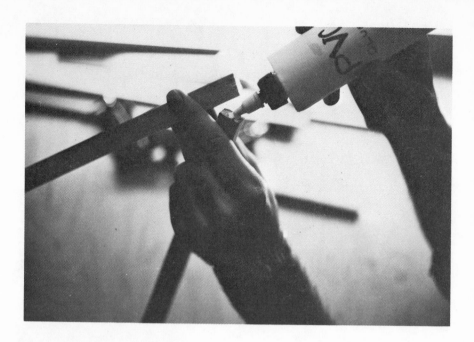

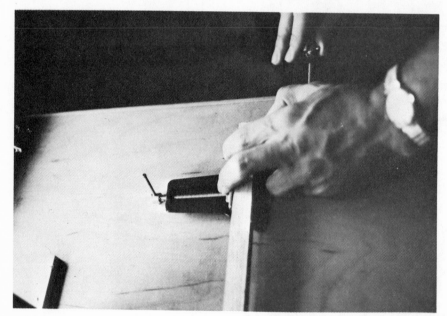

Fig. 77. (Top) Glue a short and a long side together. Be sure the long side overlaps the short side.

Fig. 78. (Center) Clamp the sides in the framing clamp. Make sure both pieces are flat against the bottom of the clamp. Alternate tightening each side bit by bit; the surfaces will be brought firmly together.

Fig. 79. (Bottom) Nail the corner together using 1½-inch brads. The first brad is driven about ¼-inch from the top of the frame and about ¼-inch from the outside. The second brad is driven lower and toward the inside. Repeat Figs. 78 through 80 for the other long and short side. Repeating the same steps twice, combine the sections together to complete the rabbet. Later we will join it to a liner.

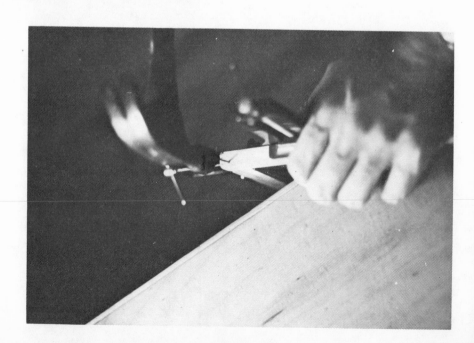

the same 8 by 10 inch picture, using 1/2 inch wide molding, you would measure the widths at 9-1/8 inches (8 plus 1/2 inch for miter allowance, plus another 1/2 inch for miter allowance, plus 1/8 inch accommodation). The total length would be 11-1/8 inches (10 plus 1/2 plus 1/2 plus 1/8).

As with the rabbet, the first short side should be cut (with a miter cut) then used as a pattern for the second short side. The long sides should be treated likewise.

The liner will be assembled in much the same way as the rabbet. But do check the dimensions by laying the liner sides on top of the rabbet to be sure the outer edges of both coincide. First, glue a long and a short side together, then place them in the framing clamp, being sure that the mitered edges match perfectly. If they are somewhat rough you can sandpaper them later. Nail two brads in the corner. Place one brad as close as possible to the inside edge of the molding and the other near the outside edge to prevent twisting. Glue and nail the other long and short sides together. Finally, glue and nail the two parts together. To join the rabbet and liner together cover the entire surface of one side of the rabbet with glue. Place the rabbet glued side down on the back of the liner. Then join the liner and rabbet with 3/4 inch brads—three or four brads to a side. You may want to cover or leaf your liner later.

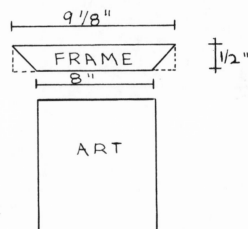

Fig. 80. When measuring for sides that have mitered corners, allow for the width of the art, plus twice the width of the molding, plus an extra ⅛-inch for accommodation.

How to Make a Frame

If you plan to use a liner it will not be necessary to add a rabbet to the outer frame since the liner already has one. Be sure that the frame molding is deep enough from front to back, so that the liner and rabbet won't be revealed when looking at the picture from the side.

To make a frame you will need the same materials and equipment as for making the liner. You might want to choose a *cove molding* or an ornate molding.

For the measurements of the outer frame you'll need either the art measurements or, if you've made a liner, the liner's outer measurements. As with the liner, you'll have to take into consideration the miter edges and an extra 1/8 inch for

Fig. 81. Cut the first miter cut for the first short side of your frame after you have figured what length the side should be. The side should be the size of the art, plus twice the width of the molding, plus an extra ⅛-inch. Since the rabbet will eventually be glued to the underside of the liner, check the measurements of this first short side to be sure it will be the same length as the rabbet. Cut the second miter cut for the first short side. (Remember to cut it at the opposite 45-degree angle from the first cut.) Use the first short side as a pattern for the second short side. Repeat this step for the two long sides. Clamshell builder's molding is used in this example.

accommodation, particularly if you cover your liner with fabric. For the same 8 by 10 inch picture in a liner 9-1/8 by 11-1/8 inches, the outer frame sides would have to be cut about 13-1/4 by 15-1/4 inches, for a two inch thick molding. (Remember the 9-1/8 inch outer perimeter of the liner, plus 2 inches for miter cut, plus 2 inches for miter cut plus 1/8 inch accommodation.) However, the liner should be measured for more accurate measurement. Cut the first miter end of the first side of the frame. Then hold the mitered end against the edge of the insert and mark the first long side of the frame. It should be very close to your original figure (13-1/4 inches in this example). Cut the miter end as measured at the opposite 45-degree angle from the first miter. Do the same with the other three sides of the frame. They are now ready to be joined. Continue as with the insert. Glue, and then nail the sides together with 1-1/2 inch brads. You might want to use a nail set to drive the brads in so as to avoid scarring the wood.

If you don't plan to use a liner with the frame, now is the time to glue and nail the rabbet to the frame, as detailed in the preceding section on how to make a liner.

If you have a liner with a rabbet, join it with the finished frame after it has been covered or finished. Apply glue around the flat outside edge of the liner. Hold the frame vertically and slide the insert in from the back. To hold the frame and liner together nail 1 inch brads through the rabbet into the frame.

Fig. 82. (Top) Glue, clamp and then nail a short and long side together. Repeat with the other short and long side. Combine the two segments together.

Fig. 83. (Center) Assemble the liner and rabbet by using white glue and ¾-inch brads.

Fig. 84. (Bottom) Cover one surface of the rabbet with glue.

Fig. 85. (Top) Place the glued surface of the rabbet on the back of the liner and nail ¾-inch brads through the rabbet to the liner. Be sure the outside edges of the rabbet and liner coincide.

Fig. 86. (Center) The finished liner and rabbet are shown from the front view. It could be finished and used as a frame. However, we are going to make another outside frame to fit around this liner which we will cover with fabric.

Fig. 87. (Bottom) Materials needed to make your frame are: miter box and backsaw, C-clamps, yardstick, framing clamp, hammer, nail set, glue, 1½-inch brads, piece of molding. Cove molding is shown here.

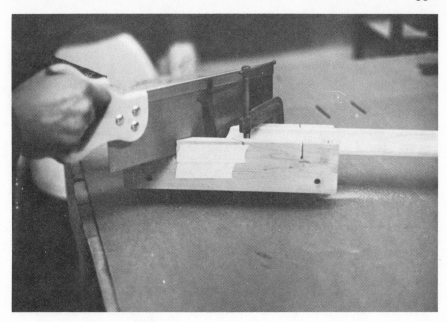

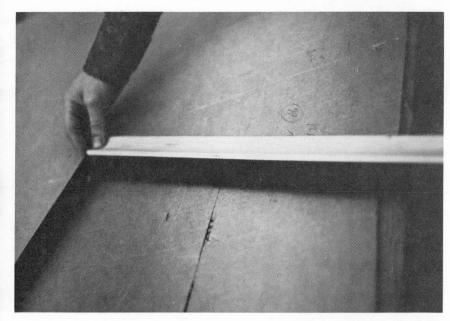

Fig. 88. (Top) Cut the first miter cut of the first short side. Calculate the length of this side.

Fig. 89. (Center) Double check this measurement by placing it against the liner. Make the second cut on the first side at an opposite 45-degree angle.

Fig. 90. (Bottom) Sand lightly any rough spots on the edges. You might also do this after the frame is assembled.

Fig. 91. (Top) Glue, then clamp the first short and long sides together.

Fig. 92. (Center) Nail the section together with 1½-inch brads. Repeat with the remaining short and long sides.

Fig. 93. (Bottom) Combine the two segments by glueing, clamping then nailing for the finished frame. You may want to use a nail set to drive the brads below the surface of the wood. When you are painting or putting a finish on the frame you will then apply wood filler to close the holes made by the brads.

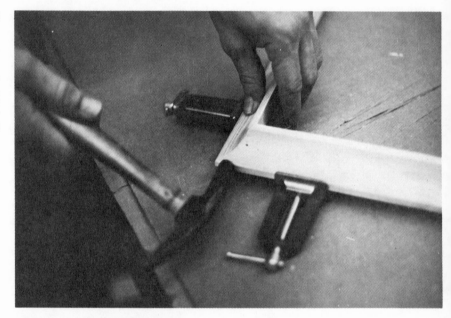

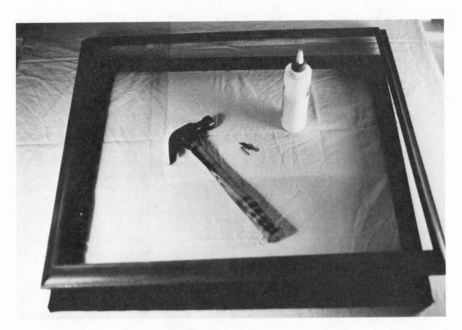

Fig. 94. (Above) Materials needed for joining a liner and frame are: hammer, 1-inch brads and glue. In this example the liner has been covered with black fabric and the frame has been given an antique finish.

Fig. 95. (Below) Apply a thin, even coat of glue to the outside edge of the liner.

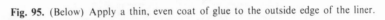

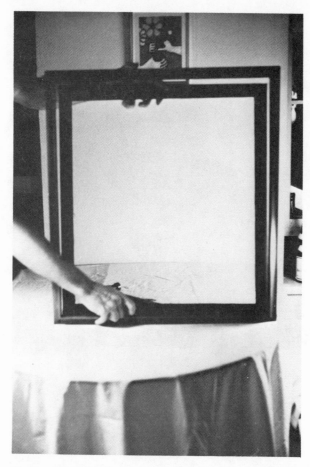

Fig. 96. (Above) Place the liner into the frame. Be sure it is evenly inserted entirely around the frame.

Fig. 97. (Below) Drive brads through the rabbet into the outer frame. Begin by driving one brad into each side. Check to see that the liner is properly positioned. Then drive in brads about every four or five inches.

Fig. 98. (Above) The frame and liner are ready to receive the art.

Fig. 99. (Below) The framing clamp is made of simple materials. This one holds a frame in place.

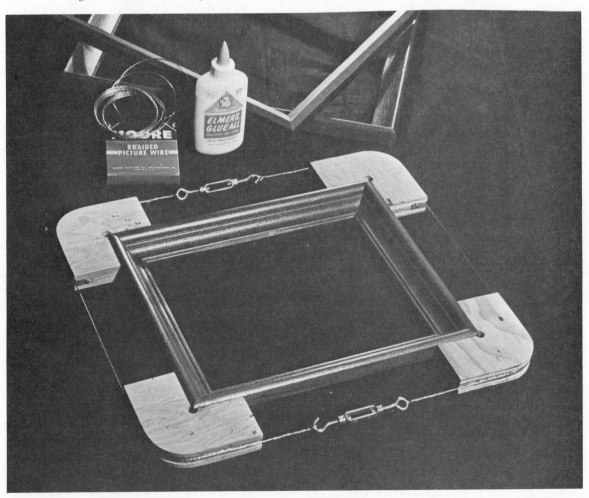

Another Type of Framing Clamp

Another type of picture framing clamp permits the joining of four corners of a frame simultaneously, without using brads in the mitered joint. The clamp shown here with directions utilizes two turnbuckles, a strand of strong picture hanging wire and four corner blocks as adapted from an article in *Popular Science Magazine*.

After the frame ends have been mitered, dab white glue at each joint. Then tighten the turnbuckles and let the frame stand for half an hour. If working on a larger frame, you may want to drill holes and insert dowels in the corners for needed support.

1. Cut and shape the corner blocks 4 inches square from 3/4 inch plywood.
2. Drill 3/8 inch diameter hole in the center of each block before cutting the short 2 inch sides.
3. Make a groove for holding the wire 1/16 inch deep and 1/4 inch wide. Use a table saw to make multiple cuts.
4. Fasten the sheet metal band with 1/2 inch brads to allow the wire to slide and tighten without biting the wood.

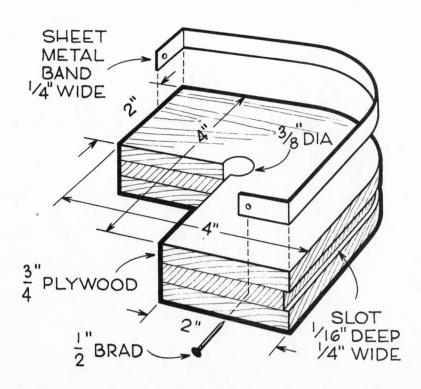

Fig. 100. The corner blocks are made from ¾-inch plywood, a sheet metal band and ½-inch brads.

Combination Moldings

By combining moldings two or more at a time you can create many different frame styles. Completely different looking frames can be constructed with the same molding or the same combination, by placing the molding in different positions; a frame can be made by joining *drip cap* together so the thickest side is visible.

Combining builder's moldings not only enlarges the number of different types of frames that can be created, it makes massive frames more readily available at a lower cost. A combination molding also helps protect against warpage. By applying various finishes to the different moldings in a combination, you can produce a frame that suits your art in all ways—in colors, textures and proportions. The illustrations given here indicate a few combinations of moldings possible. Think how many other combinations can be made by simply repositioning the moldings and applying various colors and textures.

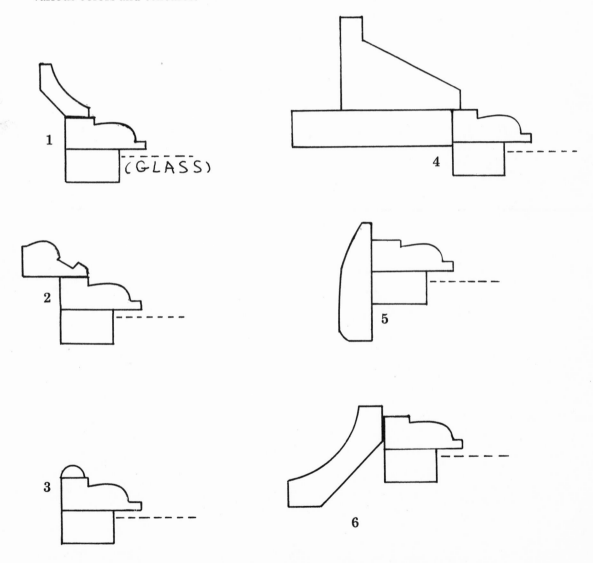

Fig. 101. Beginning with colonial dado molding and a parting strip, new frame designs can be formed by adding another molding. Here combination moldings are made with: 1) cove molding, 2) ogee molding, 3) half round molding, 4) drip cap and 1" by 4", 5) clamshell molding, and 6) large cove molding is added in a different position from No. 1.

Chapter 7

Finishing and Refinishing Frames

The final choice—the culmination of your own artistic endeavors—is the choice of a frame finish. There are many color and textural effects available. These allow you to indulge your creative talents to the utmost. However, as with your previous choices of mats, liners and frame design, the finish should blend with your picture.

A picture with a strong geometric pattern and texture might be enhanced by a frame made of combined moldings—perhaps each in a different texture.

For a picture done in the style of the old masters, you might refinish an antique frame and simply give it a coat of gray patina and a slight color glaze that complements the picture.

You can gold leaf a narrow lip of a frame, make gouges and grooves in a broad area or apply a spatter effect to part or all of your frame. The color and textural combinations you can produce are as varied as your creative force allows. The real fun in picture framing is about to begin—texturing and toning your frame.

Wood for Frames

The frame made of cove builder's molding, photographed in Chapter 6 is made of pine. Most builder's molding is made of pine, most of which is a *softwood*. Softwoods have a rather nondescript grain and are good woods to cover with texture, color or gold leaf.

Hardwoods, such as walnut and cherry, are often found in antique frames. The wood has a lovely grain. The grain of these frames should be brought out by oil and varnish finishes.

Tools and Materials You'll Need

Tools you'll need for giving your frames texture can be collected from various areas of your household. To give a frame texture, either cut into its surface or add to its surface. Any tool that helps you do either—in an interesting fashion—is an asset.

One important item to use after nearly every procedure is sandpaper. It helps remove wood "burrs" and softens and smooths gouges and textural treatments when desired. Proper use of sandpaper can mean the difference between a good job and a great one. Sandpaper also helps remove the top coat of color so that the undercoat can show in small areas to produce interesting nuances. Or it can remove metal leaf in places so the undercoat of color acrylic can show. After you have sanded each area, go over it with cheesecloth to remove the loose particles.

Other tools that can be used to give texture to your frames are: palette knife, wood rasp, triangular file, ice pick, screw driver, upholsterer's jute webber and hair comb. The use of such tools will be discussed as we continue.

Tools you'll need to color the frame are sandpaper or steel wool, a brush, cheesecloth, gold leaf and its brush, rubber gloves and whatever base coats and finishing application you desire—be it oil, varnish or color.

Preparing the Surface

At this time, fill the holes made by the brads with wood filler. You might also fill any little gaps in the mitered corners of the frame. Be sure that the holes are solidly filled, then level off the filler. When it has dried, sand the areas where filler was used with 220 grade sandpaper.

Next, "scuff" the entire frame. That is, sand it so that succeeding applied finishes will adhere. Use a coarse grade of sandpaper. Brush away particles that remain with cheesecloth. The frame is ready for oil, stain, acrylic lacquer or other finishes to be applied.

Giving Your Frame Texture

Textural effects are usually made before coloring the frame. They can be made by burning, raking, rasping, gouging, texturing gesso, and texturing modeling paste to name a few ways. Using the equipment suggested earlier you can bring about a variety of effects to be used by themselves or in combination.

RAKING the wood means making a number of indentations along the frame the way a yard rake would do if it were dragged across sand. To make these indentations you might sharpen the prongs of a fork or use an upholstery jute webber or sharp instrument like an ice pick. You might also make the rake by filing V-shaped teeth into the edge of a paint scraper with a triangular file. By making the teeth uneven, you can give the frame a more natural appearance. Begin at the miters of your prepared frame and rake with the grain from the miter to the center if possible. Then sand the surface lightly to remove excess burrs. You might then finish the frame with stain or color.

Fig. 102. The pattern in the frame on the left can be made by raking the frame. The indentations are made by a sharp instrument being drawn across the frame sides. The lip of the frame on the right was textured with a wood rasp. The rasp was drawn lightly at a diagonal angle over the lip. These patterns work well together.

RASPING a wood frame is very effective, particularly when the work is done on elevated lips and ridges. Hold the wood rasp flat and bring it diagonally across the surface to make a row of ridges. Sand, and then brush away particles. This effect works well in conjunction with the raking method.

TEXTURING GESSO is another way of making a striking texture for your frame. For this process you can use an actual manufactured gesso available at your art supply store, a thick undiluted white vinyl base paint, or acrylic modeling paste. The gesso or its substitute seals and serves as a painting ground as well as affording a fine texturing medium for the frame. For applying the gesso you'll need a brush and a pocket comb or a comb made from cardboard. Brush on a thick coat of gesso and let it dry until it will retain a scratch without filling in. Draw the comb across the partially dried gesso. You can create different textures by drawing the comb across the frame once, or back and forth a number of times in a number of ways—experiment.

There are an infinite number of different textures to be created with gesso. But once more, we caution you—keep in mind, while you've having the fun of discovering various textures, that the frame is to harmonize with the picture and should not upstage it.

Fig. 103. Gesso was applied to this frame then allowed to dry somewhat until it could retain an indentation without filling. A pocket comb or other instrument can be drawn across the gesso to give it texture.

CRACKLE surfacing is available in either clear or white at paint stores. It should be sprayed or brushed on before coloring the frame. It is then allowed to dry and crackle. Color is applied directly over it.

Giving Color to Your Frame

Let's begin with OILS—those most natural of finishes. Oils are used to bring out the natural grain and color of fine woods. The most common oil used is *linseed oil*. It can be rubbed into the wood with rags. Besides being a beautifier, it preserves the wood. Linseed oil should be rubbed into the frame several times, allowing the frame 12 to 18 hours to dry between applications. After the initial applications, it should be applied every six to twelve months.

WOOD STAINS give the frame a dark wood tone or color tone. They can be applied directly to the sanded frame after it has been prepared. The more stain applied, the darker the tone becomes. Staining requires no further finish.

Several shades of PATINAS are essential to the frame finisher. Patinas provide a finish on raw wood and also can be used to give an antique effect when applied over other colors and over metallic leaf. Two shades—a warm and a cool patina—are often made in quantity and stored. The warm patina can be made by mixing black acrylic and raw umber acrylic to white acrylic paint so as to get a medium-light grey base. Then, the adding of yellow ochre and red results in a warm, brownish-grayish patina. To make the cool patina, begin with the medium-light gray base, made from black, raw umber and white. Then add a small amount of ultramarine blue (not enough to "blue" the color—just enough to "cool" it). The patinas are a beginning point for many frame finishes.

PAINTS are applied with a brush in short, light strokes going with the wood's grain as much as possible. Paint should dry thoroughly between coats. Each coat should be sanded then brushed to remove particles. Acrylic paints that come in tubes may have to be diluted with water.

VARNISHES are available in matte or gloss finishes. They should be clear. The application of varnishes differs with each type, so be sure to read the directions. When varnishing the frame, begin in the middle and brush with short, light, even strokes to the corners. Each coat should be allowed to dry, rubbed with sandpaper, then brushed with cheesecloth.

SPATTER can be applied to a frame that already has an over-all coat of finish. Use a toothbrush to apply the spatter. Dip the toothbrush in a colored acrylic and rub a pencil across it so the bristles will bend and fling the paint on the frame. Be sure to practice this technique on newspaper before you try it on your frame. You may want to discharge the first load of paint on a newspaper each time you dip your toothbrush to insure that the excess paint does not run instead of spatter.

GILDING is the master framer's finish—it's perhaps the most luxurious and hardest to achieve of the finishes. There is *one* very complicated process of applying leaf in the traditional manner. Following is a much simplified way that produces fine results. Materials and tools needed include: gold leaf and brush, paint brush, acrylic gesso, # 220-grade sandpaper, red acrylic paint, acrylic medium, burnisher, paint scraper, orange shellac, alcohol and varnish.

After the frame is prepared, two or three coats of acrylic gesso should be applied then smoothed with a # 220-grade sandpaper. Red acrylic paint should be brushed over the gesso. (You might want to apply ochre, or perhaps a blue acrylic here as a cooler tone.) Immediately before the gold leaf is applied, a coating of acrylic medium should be applied with a brush. A measured amount of gold leaf, wider than the frame or part to be covered, should be scored with your fingernail. The piece is lifted on the brush and gently placed on the acrylic coated wood. The frame is then burnished carefully. It can be physically antiqued if desired, by lightly tapping the frame with a paint scraper or other instrument. The frame is then given a coat of orange shellac. In another method of creating antique effect some leaf can be rubbed away with alcohol to show the color underneath. Varnish can then be applied to protect the finish. Before the varnish is applied you may want to apply another alcohol wash or casein wash or rub the frame with steel wool to allow more color to show.

A much easier way to get a somewhat similar effect is to use WAX GILDING. For this you will need patina, paste wax, bronzing powder, a paint pan and some rags. Begin by applying patina to the frame. Next rub some wax in bronzing powder that has been poured into the paint pan. Then rub the wax gilt mixture over the frame until it is thoroughly covered. After the gilt has dried, buff the frame with a clean rag to bring out its sheen.

Fig. 104. (Left) Apply several coats of gesso. Allow each to dry and then smooth with sandpaper. (Photos for this process were taken at Julius Lowy Frame and Restoring Co., Inc. This mammoth antique frame is being enlarged. The darker portion is the older frame.)

Fig. 105. (Below) Sand either wet or dry.

Fig. 106. (Above) Brush a colored acrylic paint over the gesso. Red acrylic is most often used, but you might want a different hue depending on your picture.

Fig. 107. (Bottom, left) Brush a small amount of acrylic medium on the frame where you wish to place the gold leaf to attract it. Lift the portion of gold leaf with the gold leaf brush.

Fig. 108. (Bottom, right) Place the gold leaf on the frame overlapping the portion next to it.

Fig. 109. (Top, left) Repeat the process until the frame is covered.

Fig. 110. (Top, right) Burnish the frame. This will keep the leaf from chipping.

Fig. 111. (Below) Antique the frame if you wish by making indentations. This can be done with a paint scraper.

Fig. 112. (Above) Coat the frame with orange shellac to help keep the leaf from chipping. Rub away some of the leaf with alcohol or steel wool to allow the color to show through. Apply a final protective coat of varnish.

Fig. 113. (Below) Materials needed to antique are: paint undercoat, patinas or glazes, paintbrush, sandpaper, #000 steel wool, cheesecloth and rubber gloves.

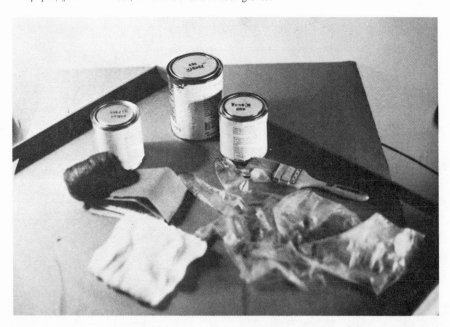

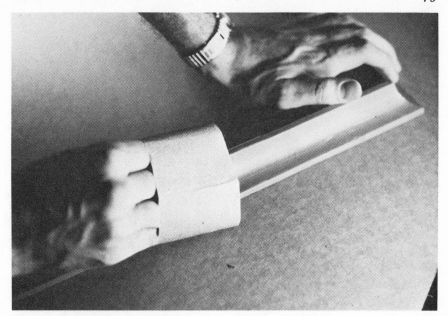

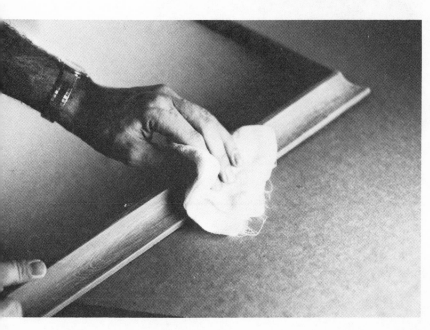

Fig. 114. (Top) Sand the frame surface to create a "scuff" so the undercoat will adhere.

Fig. 115. (Center) Remove loose particles by rubbing the frame with cheesecloth. Sanding and rubbing with cheesecloth should take place after every application of glaze.

Fig. 116. (Bottom) Apply the undercoat. This will give the frame color. Allow it to dry, then sand and brush it.

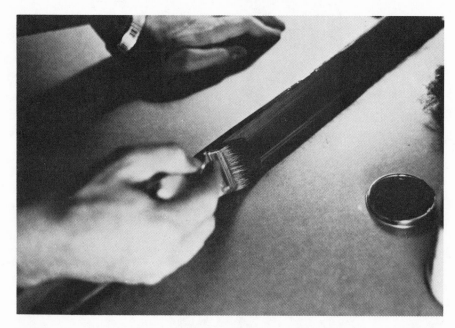

Fig. 117. (Above) Apply glazing to the frame. It should be applied in a very thin coat and should not entirely cover the undercoat. Allow the glaze to dry until it is very tacky.

Fig. 118. (Below) Rub the glaze with steel wool to allow the undercoat to show. Sand then brush with cheesecloth after the glaze has thoroughly dried. Repeat the process with another glaze if you wish.

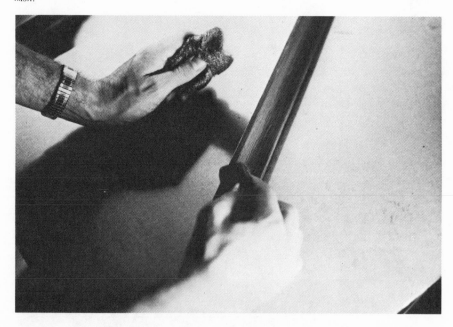

ANTIQUING can be achieved by using the patinas or a commercial antique kit. Antiquing is a fine finish to use on the frames of many pictures for its aesthetic value and as a good solution for marred frames. To antique you'll need an undercoat of paint, patinas or glazes for the antique look, paintbrush, sandpaper, # 000 steel wool for wiping and finishing, cheesecloth for dusting after sanding and protective gloves.

First, sand the frame to create a "scuff" so that the undercoat will adhere. Remove loose particles with cheesecloth. Then apply the undercoat and allow it to dry. This undercoat is a paint to hold the glazes and to give a colored background to the antiquing. A patina or a combination of patinas or glazes is applied to give the effect of wood tone shadings and antiquing. Several different tones are most effective. The glazes should be applied in a very thin coat not totally covering the undercoat. The glaze should be "poked" into crevices rather than being allowed to fill them completely. Work the glaze or patina as far as it will go before refilling your paintbrush. Sand or steel wool some of the glaze away after it has dried somewhat so the color will show. Let each coat dry thoroughly, and sand, and then rub away particles between each coat.

Refinishing Your Frames

If you enjoy the finishing part of making frames much more than constructing them, and you also like to rummage in second-hand stores and thrift shops, then refinishing old picture frames might bring you the greatest joy. Many old frames have outrageously elaborate decoration that when subdued somewhat gives a subtle elegance to the frame, and draws the observer's eye to the picture in a most pleasing manner.

After you've found a likely frame, be certain that it will—or can be reinforced to support your art. Prepare the frame by washing it with denatured alcohol to clean the surface and free it of wax and oil. Next, sand the surface with coarse sandpaper to create a "tooth" for the finish to adhere. Pay special attention to carved valleys in the frame. Fill any gaps or gouges that you don't want in the frame with wood filler. Sand the filler when it has dried. After the frame is relatively smooth it is ready to be treated with gesso for texturing, a patina, acrylic paint, gold leaf or antiquing by following the directions described in this chapter.

Chapter 8

Cut Glass — To Protect Your Picture

One way of protecting your art from the elements is by covering it with glass. Glass is used on graphics, watercolors, pastels, photographs and for items placed in shadowboxes. However, oil paintings and reproductions on linen surfaces are protected by varnish. Lithographs are protected with spray lacquer and ceramics, wood and metal sculptures are left unprotected—unless they are matted with a fabric that might easily be soiled, in which case they are covered by glass.

Types of Glass Picture Coverings

Picture glass is 1/16 inch thick—either regular or non-glare glass. It is available in varying stock sizes up to 36 by 48 inches.

NON-GLARE GLASS is treated so that there is virtually no reflection, even when it covers a picture hung in a sunny spot. However, it has several disadvantages. It has a slight tendency to distort colors and deaden whites and blacks. It also distorts the subject to a small extent, the more distortion occurring as the glass is moved farther from the subject. It is also much more expensive than regular picture glass.

A glass cutter with a cutting wheel is used to cut the glass. It is fairly inexpensive and is usually replaced when the cutter becomes dull. To prevent rusting you might keep the wheel in kerosene. To insure a good cut, dip the wheel in kerosene before each incision.

Before you begin cutting glass for your picture you should practice your cutting on strips of glass, until you can make a cut with one smooth stroke. Don't draw your cutter over the same cut more than once—it can cause the glass to shatter or give an imperfect cut.

PLEXIGLAS is an alternative to glass when the picture is to be shipped or carted a long distance. It is much stronger than glass and is virtually shatter proof. It is also cut with an inexpensive cutter. Plexiglas is expensive and is prone to scratches.

84

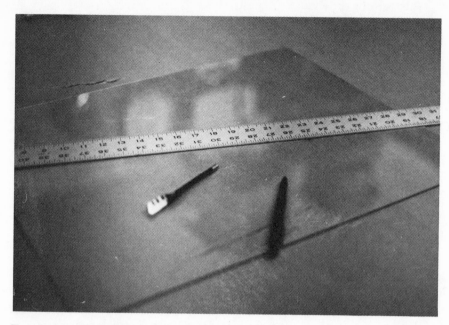

Fig. 119. (Above) Materials needed for cutting glass include the glass, a glass cutter, a pencil or grease pencil and a metal yardstick.

Fig. 120. (Below) Measure and mark off the dimensions that you want your glass to be. It should be the size of the mat and mount—about ⅛ inch less in length and width than the rabbet opening.

How to Cut the Glass

Begin with a flat working surface. You'll need a glass cutter, a metal ruler and a pencil. Measure the size of glass needed. It should be the same size as the mat and mount—about 1/8 inch less in length and width than the rabbet opening. Mark off the measurements with a lead or grease pencil. Then place the metal straightedge along the line to be cut. You might want to dip the cutting wheel in kerosene before cutting. This aids the cutting wheel in making a clean stroke.

Fig. 121. (Top) Cut the glass in one smooth stroke starting from the top and working toward your body. Cutter should be held firmly between the index and middle finger gripped by your thumb.

Fig. 122. (Center) Place the scored side of the glass up on the edge of the work table with the excess hanging over the table. Firmly grasp the excess edge, raise the glass slightly and crack it sharply on the table edge. The glass should snap neatly along your scoring. . .

Fig. 123. (Bottom) . . .to produce two separate pieces of glass. Be sure to wash the glass with alcohol or water and newspaper before placing it into the frame.

Hold the glass cutter firmly between the index and middle finger and grip it with your thumb. Start at the top of the glass and work toward your body. Holding your arm steady apply pressure and move the cutter in a continuous stroke downward until you have scored the glass. There should be a steady hiss as the glass is being scored.

Place the glass on the edge of the table scored side up with the excess hanging over the table. Firmly grasp the excess edge, raise the glass slightly and crack it sharply on the table edge. The glass should snap neatly along your scoring.

If the glass doesn't snap neatly along the score, turn the glass over and tap it with the handle of your glass cutter along the score, then turn it back over and try snapping it again.

Remember to clean the backside of your glass before placing it in the frame. You can do this with either water or alcohol and newspaper.

Chapter 9

Get It Together and Hang It Up!

Now is the time to cut and gather the final elements of your frame and assemble them into the finished product. With the exception of paintings done on canvas and reproductions of them, frames for most types of art are assembled in much the same way.

Assembling Framed Canvases

A painting done on a canvas differs from other art in that it doesn't require glass, is usually placed into covered liners and is painted on canvas that is fastened to stretcher bars. Therefore, assembling its frame (and frames for good reproductions that should be treated in the same manner as the original) is somewhat different from putting together frames for other types of art.

After the liner(s) and frame are glued and nailed together, the canvas—still on stretcher bars—is fitted into the inner liner's rabbet. Long nails are driven at an angle through the stretcher bars and into the rabbet. Be sure when you are making a frame for a canvas that the rabbet is deep enough to accommodate the stretcher bars.

Brown wrapping paper is dampened and glued around the perimeter of the stretcher bars, then trimmed and dried. Although backing board is usually used between the mount and the wrapping paper, it is eliminated with canvases which need air.

Fig. 124. Materials needed to hang your picture are: mounted and matted art, frame, glass, backing board (double-faced corrugated backing is good), X-acto knife, yardstick, pair of pliers, adhesive tape, scissors, ice pick, wrapping paper, glue, screw eyes and picture wire (or hanging device) and 3/4 inch brads.

Materials You'll Need for Framing Other Art

Besides your art secured in a mat or mats, frame and glass, you'll need backing board (double-faced corrugated backing is fine), cut to the size of the glass and mount, X-acto knife, yardstick, pair of pliers, adhesive tape, scissors, ice pick, wrapping paper, glue, screw eyes and picture wire (or a hanging device) and 3/4 inch brads.

Assembling the Finished Product

After the corrugated backing board has been cut to the size of the glass and mount, you will be ready to assemble the frame's components. There is nothing more distressing after all your labors than to see a speck of something between the glass and art; so be sure to clean the glass thoroughly and check at intervals to see that the mat and art are lint free.

Place the clean glass, matted picture and backing into the frame's rabbet. After they have been placed check to see that there is no lint on the mat or picture and no fingerprints on the inside of the glass. The rabbet should project higher than the backing.

With your pliers squeeze 3/4 inch brads into the rabbet. The brads will hold the backing and other components in the frame. Wrap masking tape around the plier grip that presses against the outside of the frame so the frame won't be marred. Place one brad in each side of the rabbet, then check the picture again for lint and positioning. If everything is in order, squeeze the rest of the brads into the rabbet at three to four inch intervals.

Use the brown wrapping paper to cover the back of the picture. Cut a piece about one inch larger on all sides than the frame. Dampen the paper with the rags. This will cause the paper to expand slightly before it is glued on the back of the frame. When the paper dries it will contract to its former size and will be a taut, smooth cover.

Spread an even coat of glue around the back edge of the frame and place the damp wrapping paper on it. Smooth the paper over the back of the frame.

Allow the paper to dry and become tight. Then with your yardstick trim it about 1/4 inch in from the outside edge of the frame.

Next, the hanging device is attached. It may take the form of a decorative hanger placed on top of the picture frame. More often, picture screw eyes are attached to the back of the frame and strung with picture hanging wire. To locate screw placement for small and medium sized pictures—which need only two screw eyes—simply measure and mark the distance one-third of the way down from the top of the frame.

To make it easier to start the screw eyes, spike a hole with the ice pick. Then twist the screw eyes with your fingers or a pair of pliers. Loop the picture hanging wire twice through one screw eye. Twist about three inches of the wire back around itself. The wire strung between the screw eyes should not be taut, otherwise it will not reach the wall hook. However, it should not have so much slack that the picture top tips away from the wall when hung. Cut the wire so there will be a three inch excess after it is brought twice through the second screw eye. Again twist the wire back on itself.

Wire for large pictures should be strung using four screw eyes as shown in the photographs.

Driving Picture Hanging Nails Into Your Walls

When you drive picture hanging nails into a plaster wall, place a square of masking tape with some of its adhesive removed to the wall and drive the nail into it. The adhesive quality of the tape will prevent the plaster from cracking. Be sure you remove some of the adhesive quality before you apply the tape on the wall. Otherwise the tape might take some of the paint with it when removed.

Fig. 125. Place glass (none is used in this example since it is a reproduction of an oil), matted picture and backing into the frame's rabbet. Be sure to check that there is no lint on mat or art.

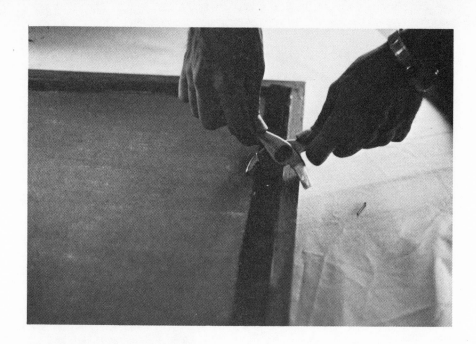

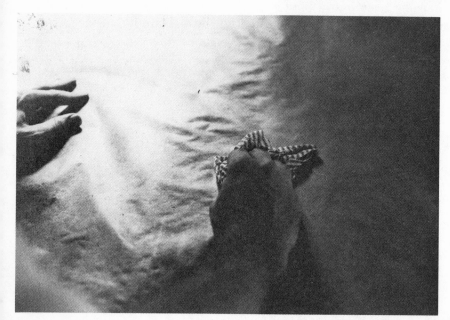

Fig. 126. (Top) Squeeze the ¾-inch brads into the rabbet with pliers. The brads will hold the backing in place. To protect the frame wrap masking tape around the plier grip that presses against the outside of the frame.

Fig. 127. (Center) Dampen the wrapping paper with a cloth. The paper should be cut about one inch larger than the frame on all sides. When the paper dries it will contract to its former size and will be a taut, smooth, dustproof cover for the back of the picture.

Fig. 128. (Bottom) Spread an even coat of glue on the back edge of the frame where the wrapping paper will adhere.

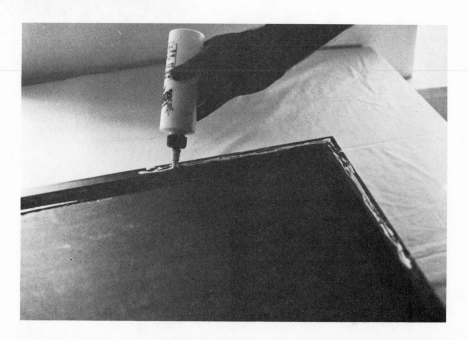

Fig. 129. (Top) Place the damp paper on the frame back and smooth it. As the paper dries it will tighten.

Fig. 130. (Center) Trim the excess paper from the back of the picture after the paper has dried somewhat. Use the yardstick and the X-acto knife to trim evenly about ¼-inch from the edge of the frame. Do not wait for the glue to dry completely, or it will be difficult to remove the excess paper.

Fig. 131. (Bottom) Locate the position for your screw eyes by measuring about one-third down from the top of the frame. Additional screw eyes will be used on the bottom of this large picture. Spike a hole with the icepick to make screwing the eyes in easier.

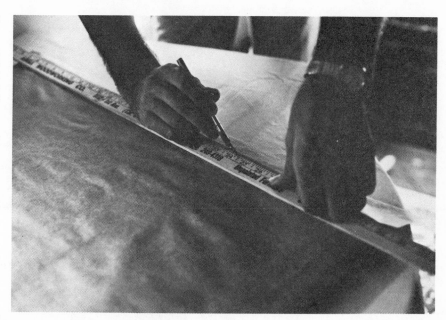

Fig. 132. (Top) Screw the eyes in the frame.

Fig. 133. (Center) Wire the picture by allowing the wire to pass freely through the side screw eyes. The wire passes through the bottom screw eyes twice and the remaining wire is twisted back on itself about 3 inches. Leave a bit of slack to allow the wire to reach the wall hook.

Fig. 134. (Bottom) Hang your picture on the wall at eye level. When driving a nail in the wall (you might use two nails for larger pictures) apply adhesive tape with some of the adhesive removed to the wall. This will protect the wall plaster from cracking.

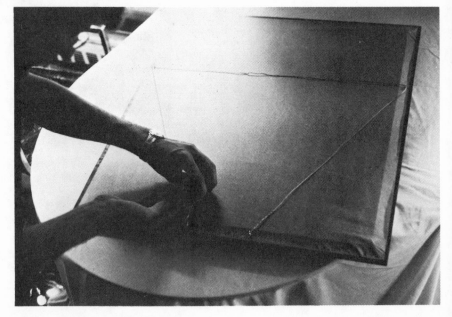

Chapter 10

Make Your Own Plastic Frames

As you've noted in Chapter 3, there are a variety of ready-made frames available in plastic. You can also make your own plastic frames in a number of different styles to suit your works of art. The equipment needed is minimal, inexpensive—and for the most part, you can use tools that you already have. Plastic frames seem to be an easily explained consequence of the plastic age—where furniture and industry and household objects are being manufactured from plastic. Plastic frames also seem to be the natural accessory to go with these furnishings. The frames are quite durable and inexpensive.

Acrylic is perhaps the most common plastic used in crafts and picture framing. It is a synthetic resin produced in sheets, tubes and rods with the application of pressure and heat. Acrylic comes in many colors and can be sprayed with color. Some widely known trade names for the material are Plexiglas, Lucite and Acrylite. In this chapter we will explore the possibilities of making picture frames from acrylic sheets—specifically, from Plexiglas. Regardless of the trade name, acrylic sheeting, tubing and rods are fashioned into products in much the same way.

Clear acrylic frames not only protect the art, but are a complete structure that houses the art and serves as a frame. Indeed, acrylic is the frame, glass and mat all in one.

Acrylic frames are compatible with a number of different types of art. Their clean, simple look makes them suitable for framing certain photographs, some modern art and diplomas and certificates. Still-life drawings and paintings and acrylic frames are often harmonious. Because of their sleek look, acrylic frames are not good selections for elegant or older art subjects. The art subject and style should be considered when thinking about a plastic frame as a framing option.

The Acrylic "Plexiglas"

The popularity of acrylic sheet as a material for home projects is rapidly growing ... the name Plexiglas is often heard among home project enthusiasts. Following are instructions for making several Plexiglas frames—a simple wall frame and a more complicated table frame. Also included is an idea for making a display box or model cover. Plans for projects and the tools required to make them are available from plastics dealers, hobby shops and hardware stores.

Although two formulations of Plexiglas are readily available at retail dealers, Plexiglas G is the material used in most craft work. It is the material suggested for the following projects.

While working with Plexiglas it is important to keep the protective paper covering on it. Otherwise the Plexiglas is susceptible to scratching.

Make a Plexiglas Wall Frame and Mat

This easy-to-make Plexiglas frame is ideal for bathroom or kitchen. The picture is sandwiched between the wall and the Plexiglas, protected from bathroom steam and kitchen grease. The technique for making the frame is fairly simple. You can practice making this one, then progress to more complicated frames such as the table frame project that follows. The mat around this collection of pictures is acrylic spray paint directly applied to the Plexiglas.

Fig. 135. This wall frame has its own mat spray painted directly onto the Plexiglas. The frame is a handy means of hanging a set of pictures.

Materials needed are hand scribing tool, metal straightedge, 3/4-inch wood dowel (or a power saw in place of all of preceding), hand or electric drill, sharpened piece of metal (like a knife or the *back* of a hacksaw blade) or medium grit (60-80) "production paper," 150-320-grade sandpaper "wet or dry," 400-500-grade sandpaper "wet or dry," Dico Buffing Kit for Plexiglas or clean muslin wheel dressed with good grade of fine-grit buffing compound, and oil- or acrylic-based paint (not water-base).

1. CUT a piece of 1/8 inch Plexiglas to the dimensions you'll need. (Do not remove the protective paper covering.) You can do this by hand by scribing the Plexiglas with a special Plexiglas cutting tool (Plastic Plus Cutting Tool). Place your straightedge where you want to scribe, and with firm pressure, draw the cutting point the full width of the material. Repeat 5 to 6 times. To break the Plexiglas, POSITION it over a 3/4 inch dowel running the length of the intended

break—scribed side up. Hold the sheet with one hand and APPLY DOWNWARD PRESSURE on the side containing the smallest piece of material with the other hand. Reposition your hands along the scribed line about 2 inches in back of the break as it progresses.

You can also cut the Plexiglas with a power saw—sabre, band and reciprocating jig saws or circular saws, in which case you can cut circular and curved frames. Just remember not to remove the protective paper before cutting. Sabre and reciprocating jig saws should have 32 teeth per inch for 1/8 inch Plexiglas. Band saws should have at least 10 teeth per inch. Circular saws should have the Cope RH-600 or RH-800 circular saw blade for Plexiglas or a steel crosscut blade recommended for finish cuts on plywood, veneers, laminates, etc. The blade should have at least 6 teeth per inch. All teeth should be of the same shape, height and point-to-point distance, and blade height should be set somewhat above the thickness of the sheet to prevent chipping.

Plexiglas should be held down firmly when cutting. It should not be force fed.

2. DRILL four holes for screws to fasten picture to the wall. You can do this with a hand drill or electric drill. When using a standard twist drill commonly used for metals, back the Plexiglas with wood, clamp or hold it firmly, and use a sharp drill *at a very low speed and with minimum pressure.* If too much speed is used, the Plexiglas will tend to climb the drill. Too much pressure might cause chipping.

To drill Plexiglas sheet with electric equipment, special drills like the Hanson Special Purpose High Speed Twist Drills are required. Tighten the drill securely in the chuck. Back the Plexiglas sheet with soft wood and clamp or hold firmly. Use the highest speed available up to 3000 rpm. However, if you drill holes 3/8 inch or larger use a slower speed (1000-2000 rpm). Do not force feed.

3. FINISH the edges of your wall frame. There are three stages to edge finishing: smooth finish, satin finish and transparent finish.

The smooth finish removes sawed edges and other tool marks. Rounding corners and smoothing uneven cuts can be done by filing with a medium to fine tooth metal file. File, saw and other tool marks are easily removed by scraping the edge with a sharpened piece of metal such as the *back* of a hacksaw blade, or sanding with medium grit (60-80) "production paper."

The satin finish improves the appearance of the edge and (although in this project we will not cement Plexiglas together) prepares it for cementing. To get the satin finish, sand Plexiglas with increasingly finer grades (150-320) of "wet or dry paper." Also, when cementing Plexiglas together, take care not to round the edge sides in this step because it will result in bubbles in the cemented joint.

The third finish—the transparent finish—provides a high-gloss edge. To obtain this finish continue sanding with finer grades (400-500) "wet or dry paper," then buff the edge using the Dico Buffing Kit for Plexiglas or other clean muslin wheel dressed with a good grade of fine grit buffing compound.

4. MARK the dimensions of the picture centered on the protective paper with pencil and straightedge. With a mat knife and straightedge CUT along the marked line. REMOVE the outer perimeter of protective paper which is the width your painted mat will be. The protective paper should remain on the center area where you will place your picture.

5. SPRAY the exposed Plexiglas with oil-based or acrylic-based paint. Allow it to dry.

6. When dry, REMOVE the protective covering from the center, PLACE your picture in the clear opening, SECURE it with masking tape and SCREW the finished product to the wall.

Make a Plexiglas Table Frame

Copyright Rohm and Haas Co., 1972.

This contemporary, free-standing frame involves many of the processes previously described, plus a process called "strip-heat forming." This involves thoroughly heating, then bending the Plexiglas along a straight line.

The materials you will need are the same as is needed for the Wall Frame, plus a strip heater element, the "Briskeat RH-36," and a China marker. This inexpensive heating element will allow you to heat the Plexiglas so you can bend it. The heating element rests on a base you can make from plywood, asbestos paper and aluminum foil.

1. CUT a piece of 1/8-inch Plexiglas, 8 by 22-1/2 inches for an 8 by 10 inch vertical frame. This can be done in any of the ways described in Step No. 1 of the wall frame.

2. FINISH all the edges to transparency similar to Step No. 3 of the wall frame directions.

3. REMOVE the protective masking paper.

4. Using a China marker, MARK a distance of 8 inches from the top of the piece of Plexiglas. This 8 inches will be bent over to become the back of the picture frame.

5. PLACE the Plexiglas on a strip heater element. Allow the material to heat thoroughly (until it softens or wilts in the area to be formed—about 10 to 15 minutes). BEND the Plexiglas gently and fold it back on itself. (Always bend the Plexiglas away from the side that was placed on the heater.)

6. FORM a platform on which to rest the picture by measuring off 4 inches across the width from the opposite end or bottom of the Plexiglas. Use a China marker to mark.

7. Strip HEAT the marked area and BEND it approximately 60 degrees away from the face of the frame.

With two bendings you have made a simple and attractive picture frame.

Fig. 136. (Top) Measure a piece of ⅛-inch-thick Plexiglass 8 by 22½ inches for an 8 by 10-inch vertical frame.

Fig. 137. (Center) Scribe the Plexiglas with a Plexiglas cutter. This can be done by first making a light guide line, go over it 5 or 6 times. Be sure that the very top of the material has been scribed through.

Fig. 138. (Bottom) Break the Plexiglas over a ¾-inch dowel. The Plexiglas should have its scribed side up. Apply downward pressure to the Plexiglas on either side of the dowel. You might want to cut the protective paper along the scribed side with a knife before you begin to separate the Plexiglas portions.

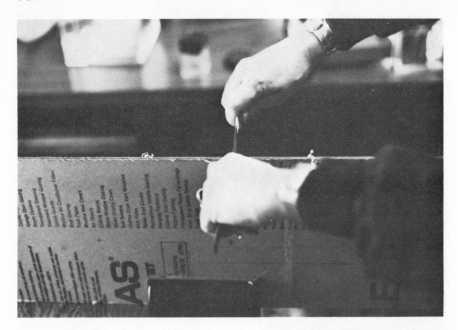

Fig. 139. (Top) Finish the edgbs to a smooth finish. The smooth finish is the first of three finishes. It is achieved by scraping the edges with a sharp piece of metal such as a knife or the back of a hacksaw blade, or sanding with medium grit production paper. The smooth finish removes sawed edges and other tool marks.

Fig. 140. (Center) Finish the edges to a satin finish. This finish further improves the appearances of the edges. Sand the Plexigas with increasingly finer grades (150-320) of "wet or dry" sandpaper.

Fig. 141. (Bottom) Finish to a transparent finish. This transparent finish provides a high gloss edge. Sand with finer grades (400-500) "wet or dry" sandpaper, then buff the edge with a Dico Buffing Kit for Plexiglas or other clean muslin wheel dressed with a good grade of fine grit buffing compound.

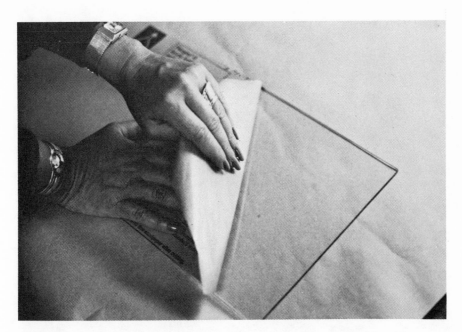

Fig. 142. (Above) Remove the protective paper. You may want to clean the Plexiglas with soap and water and a soft cloth to get rid of dust particles and static electricity.

Fig. 143. (Below) Mark a distance of 8 inches from the top of the Plexiglas with a China marker. The 8 inches will be bent over to become the back of the picture frame.

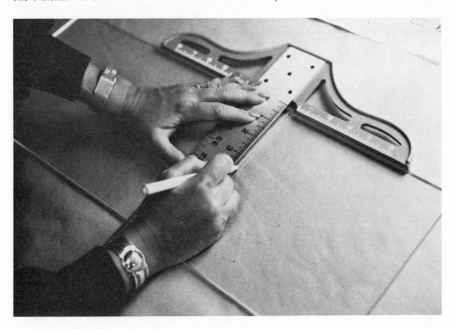

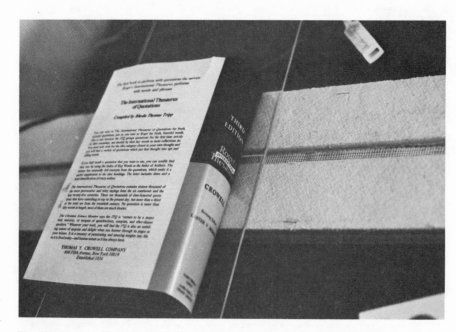

Fig. 144. (Above) Place the marked area of the Plexiglas on the strip heater. (As the Plexiglas becomes warm it has a tendency to bow upward, so you might want to place a book over it to keep it flat.) Allow the Plexiglas to soften—10 to 15 minutes.

Fig. 145. (Below) Bend the Plexiglas gently and fold it back on itself. Bend the Plexiglas away from the side it was placed on the heater.

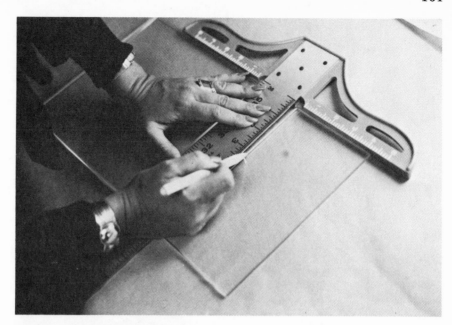

Fig. 146. (Top) Form a platform to rest the picture by measuring off 4 inches across the width from the opposite end or bottom of the Plexiglas.

Fig. 147. (Center) Heat the marked area on the strip heater.

Fig. 148. (Bottom) Bend the Plexiglas so the platform rests about 60 degrees away from the back of the frame.

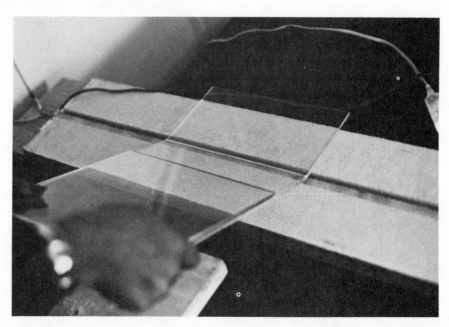

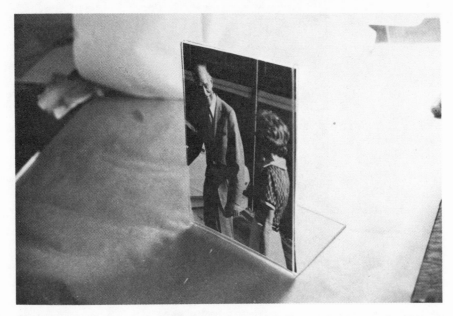

Fig. 149. Insert your picture and the job is completed. It isn't necessary to secure it with tape.

Make a Display Box

This Plexiglas display box or model cover can be used to protect many large collections from dirt and accidents while displaying them effectively. Plans for the model cover can be obtained from the materials manufacturer. The display box incorporates several techniques used on acrylic sheeting that have not been used in the previous projects: cementing Plexiglas together and drilling holes to apply a finishing band.

Various cements can be used for cementing Plexiglas. For example, IPS Weld-On #3 Solvent for Cementing Plexiglas, methylene chloride (MDC), ethylene dichloride (EDC) or 1-1-2 trichlorethane. These can be used on Plexiglas G which is suggested for craft uses. To cement two pieces together the Plexiglas edges should not be finished to the transparent stage, but cemented at the satin finish stage. The protective masking paper should be removed, and the two pieces to be joined should be held together by masking tape. Apply the solvent to the joint keeping the joint horizontal, so the force of gravity will allow the solvent to go into the joint. Let it dry thoroughly. Thickened cements are also available and can be good for mending and filling in scratches.

To add a finishing strip such as the one shown in the picture, drill a 1/16-inch oversize hole every foot along the display case, following the drilling procedure already mentioned. The holes should be located to provide at least 1/4 inch solid material from the edge of the hole to the edge of the sheet. Smooth the hole surface with a round file to provide resistance to breakage. Then tighten screws snugly—and back them off 1/4 turn to provide freedom of movement for expansion or contraction of the Plexiglas.

Fig. 150. This model cover can display antiques, collections, dried flower arrangements and other showpieces. It can be made relatively easily with Plexiglas and a finishing band.

"Band" Your Plastic Frame Together

"Jewelite" is a product borrowed from the sign industry. It provides a finishing band around a picture covered with Plexiglas, Lucite or other acrylic materials. It is available in strips and is actually plastic wrapped around metal. It forms an attractive band around the picture and can be bonded to the acrylic material with a solvent cement (ethylene dichloride). The Jewelite is very pliable and can be wrapped around acrylic material cut in any shape, thereby giving a finished edge to circles and oval frames as well as whatever shape you can devise. It also has a bevel area in the center, which makes a perfect "rabbet" to hold the picture and backing. More information can be obtained from the manufacturer.

Materials you'll need for making this frame are the transparent acrylic 1/8 inch thick to cover the picture, the Jewelite plastic-metal stripping, ethylene dichloride to bond the Jewelite to the acrylic metal shears, pencil, brush or dropper and a square-cornered file.

Fig. 151. In its original use Jewelite was wrapped around acrylic to make sign letters. Now the material, which is plastic wrapped around metal, is used as a frame for acrylic covered pictures.

1. MARK off the dimensions of your picture frame on the acrylic sheet.

2. CUT it with a metal saw (for specific directions see Step No. 1 under "Make a Plexiglas Frame and Mat" in this chapter).

3. REMOVE the protective covering from the acrylic.

4. CUT the beginning of the Jewelite stripping with metal shears so that it has a perfect even edge and can be evenly joined with the end of the Jewelite strip after it has been formed around the acrylic.

5. FIT the acrylic sheet into the rabbet bevel of the Jewelite so the cut end of the Jewelite will be flush with the bottom left corner of the acrylic.

6. RUN the stripping along the bottom of the acrylic to the bottom right corner.

7. With a large file, FILE through the Jewelite plastic coating on the INNER side of the metal. This will allow the material to bend squarely.

8. CONTINUE THE STRIPPING to the top right corner and again FILE the plastic coating on the inner side of the metal. BEND the frame.

9. Following this pattern, CONTINUE toward the top left corner and finally down to the bottom left corner where you started.

10. Use the metal shears to TRIM the excess stripping, being sure that you cut squarely so the ends will join evenly.

11. LAY the acrylic into the rabbet and APPLY the solvent cement to the stripping with brush or dropper.

12. After you have PLACED your mat, picture and backing into the frame, CUT small pieces of Jewelite and BEND them to form right angles. SECURE them to the frame with solvent cement so they will hold the backing in place.

13. A PICTURE HANGER can be made from another small piece of Jewelite folded at a right angle with a hole for a wall hanger drilled into it. Secure it likewise with the solvent cement.

Once mastered, the principles for using acrylic can be applied to other projects to produce furniture, containers, and other useful items.

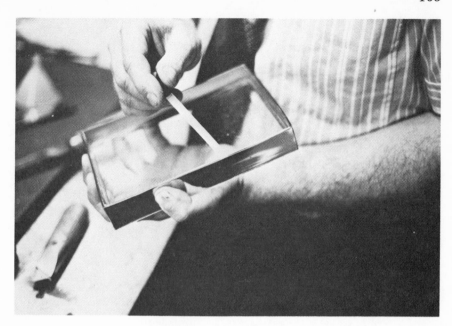

Fig. 152. (Top) After the Jewelite is bent and filed to form corners around a piece of acrylic, solvent cement is applied with eye dropper or brush. The solvent cement causes the Jewelite to adhere to the acrylic.

Fig. 153. (Center) After the matting, picture and backing are inserted into the frame, small pieces of Jewelite are bent to form right angles and secured to the frame with the solvent cement. They hold the backing in place.

Fig. 154. (Bottom) A picture hanger can be made from another small piece of Jewelite folded at a right angle with a hole drilled into it.

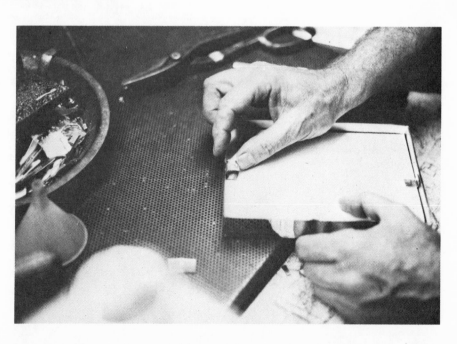

Chapter 11

Conventional Frames and Frame Mavericks

Conventional Frames

This last chapter is devoted to frame traditions and unusual frames. Both types serve as examples from which to draw your own ideas on framing creatively. Examine these and other frames—in a friend's home, in an art gallery—and let your mind soar.

The frames can be adapted according to your likes and the needs of your art. Experiment with other materials and finishing techniques. Take characteristics of several frames that would blend with your art and combine them. The more thoughtful experiment the greater your chances of success. So, let's get started.

Shadow Boxes

One of the delightful aspects of shadow boxes is that they add greatly to the number of items you can frame. If done with taste they can add distinction to the items displayed within them.

Scholarship or club pins long stored in a bureau drawer can be admired when placed in a shadow box and hung in the family room. A family collection—perhaps baby spoons or charms gathered on vacations, that have been gathering dust in the attic can be enjoyed when viewed from a shadow box.

Shadow boxes can often make thoughtful gifts. While most people like to choose the art that will be placed on their walls, a shadow box containing their mementos or one displaying objects relating to their interests can be a personal, pleasing gift. It is also a creative choice on the part of the giver.

Design considerations include choice of frame, fabric and positioning of the articles. As with picture frames, the purpose of shadow box frames is to form a focal point to attract the viewer's attention to the item(s) within the frame; the frame should have the same character as the item. Therefore, a piece of antique jewelry would be enhanced by a frame of wood grain with, perhaps, a gold leaf lip. A bright red lacquer frame might answer the need of a collection of matches gathered on the family's last camping spree along the California Coast.

Considerations in choosing fabric are color and texture. It might seem a simple task to choose a fabric color that blends attractively with the red lacquer or the wood grain frame. But also keep in mind that dark colors like black—particularly velvet—are difficult to work with because they attract lint. The texture of velvet can also be a disadvantage at times. Any holes made when securing objects to the background with nylon wire are very apt to be visible. In cases where objects must be secured, a material with a weave coarser than velvet is suggested.

Articles should be positioned in the shadow box as nearly as possible in the same way as they would be found in their natural setting. For example, a statue, rather than dangling in mid air within the shadow box, should rest on a pedestal. A pedestal can be simply fashioned from wood and painted or covered with fabric. A necklace might be hung from an attractive hook. An article assuming a natural position is a pleasing sight, although the article should be tightly secured in another manner as well.

There are several ways to engineer the shadow box depending on the size of the object, whether it will be removed from time to time and considerations particular to the object to be contained. A simple way of making a shadow box is to think of it as a very deep picture and begin from there. The parts of a simple shadow box are the frame, glass, fabric-covered background, liner covered with the same fabric as the background or painted if you wish, and the item. The size of the object from front to back determines how deep your shadow box will be.

First construct your outer frame and inner liner according to the guide lines in Chapter 6. Your frame molding should be deep enough so the rabbet in the liner won't show. You may need to add parting strip to the back of the frame to gain depth. The liner must be deep enough to separate the glass from the article. It can be painted or covered with the background fabric as described in Chapter 5. Remember its inside will be visible, and must also be painted or covered.

Glue, then carefully nail the frame and liner together with the glass separating them.

Depending upon how heavy the display items are, the background can be made of Upson board or plywood cut to fit within the liner rabbet. Remember that the fabric covering the background will take up additional depth and width, so allow for it when cutting the background. Cover the background or paint it. The technique for covering the background is similar to that for covering mats discussed in Chapter 5.

Secure the items to be displayed to the board. You might wish to countersink, then glue them, or fasten them with nylon cord. Their means of attachment should not be visible. They should be positioned on a pedestal, hook, etc.—whichever is their natural placement.

After checking that there is no lint on the background, place it in the rabbet and with a pair of pliers squeeze brads into the back of the rabbet.

Add wrapping paper backing and prepare to hang as detailed in Chapter 9.

Hand Painted Frames

Painting a pattern on your frame is another alternative for a pleasing finished effect, and another way to display your artistic talents. This handsome frame with a red velvet liner is a reproduction of a Central American Indian frame design. It frames an ink and acrylic work by Gloria Vanderbilt.

Fig. 155. This shadow box lined in reddish velvet houses a three dimensional picture. (JULIUS LOWY FRAME & RESTORING CO., INC.)

Fig. 156. An antique fan is housed in a shadow box of the same shape lined in blue taffeta. (HOUSE OF H. HEYDENRYK, JR., INC.

Papier-Mâché Frames

The papier-mâché lacquer process originated with the ancient Persians. This fine example of the process with its brilliant colors is from the Kashmir Valley.

The method might be simplified by covering a wooden frame with papier-mâché and painting, then lacquering it.

Classical Frames

These classical moldings were brought back into popularity in the United States in the 19th century. They are a natural transition from the ornate antique frames to the streamlined frames we use on much of our modern art. The frames are characterized by a raised inner and outer edge joined with a curve.

Fig. 157. This hand-painted frame is a reproduction of a Central American Indian design. (HOUSE OF H. HEYDENRYK, JR., INC.)

Fig. 158. Animals abound on this brilliantly colored papier-mache frame. The design is executed with a delicacy reminiscent of Persian miniature painting, from which this art stems.(SIAMESE IMPORTS)

Fig. 159. The forerunner of our sleek, modern frames, these classical frames are characterized by a raised inner and outer edge joined with a curve. (HOUSE OF H. HEYDENRYK, JR., INC.)

Frame Mavericks

This maverick group of frames can be divided into two divisions. First, the simplified frames or ways of hanging art were developed thanks to modern materials and innovative framing short cuts. Then what will be termed folk traditions are those frames that were popularized by hobbyists as well as artisans.

All of the frames in this group can be made with tools you probably have in your home and with materials that are readily available. They can be enjoyed for their simplicity and lack of pretension.

Framing Brackets

This temporary method of hanging already mounted and matted photographs, drawings, engravings and watercolors is fast, easy and even less expensive than the commercial brackets. An eight-foot strip of outside corner plastic molding will make brackets for eight pictures. The molding is available in several colors.

Saw the molding into six-inch strips. Drill or punch holes in the longer side of each.

Cut two pieces of cord each six inches longer than the length of the mounting board. Loop the cords through the holes of the molding and tie them.

Cover the art with glass or acrylic. Center the plastic brackets, one on the top and one on the bottom of the mounted print. Add backing if you wish.

Pass the loop of the top cord through the loop of the bottom cord, pull tightly and hang the print from the leftover loop.

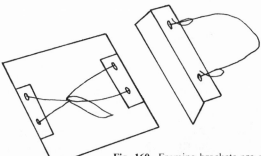

Fig. 160. Framing brackets are an easy and inexpensive way of framing art.

Passe-Partout Frames

Another inexpensive, temporary framing technique is the passe-partout method which incorporates glass or acrylic, plain backing and the mounted art, all sealed together with plastic tape.

Mount the art and cut the glass or acrylic and the backing. Attach passe-partout rings through slits in the backing. Spread the ring ends, then secure them with masking tape on the inside of the backing.

Line up the edges of the components, art faced upward, and cut a strip of tape longer than the side to be taped together. Press the tape along the edge with about 1/4-inch tape width on the front of the glass or acrylic. Smooth down the tape. Being careful to keep the elements in place, fold the tape back along the backing. Either trim off the edges of the tape evenly at the corner of the glass, or miter it. Then repeat the procedure on the opposite side. After all four sides are sealed, loop picture hanging wire through the rings.

NOTE: Both the bracket and passe-partout method can be further simplified by eliminating glass or acrylic and mat. (Do not eliminate both in the passe-partout method however, or you will be forced to apply tape to the mounted art.)

Fig. 161. Passe-partout rings are attached by passing the ring ends through slits in the frame backing, spreading the ends and securing them with masking tape.

Laminated Frames

Decorative mirrors can be made by laminating plywood—cut straight or curved with a jigsaw—with fabric or decorative paper adhered by white glue. A room with wallcovering in a gay pattern could especially benefit with a mirror in matching paper. Note the finishing braid along the plywood edges closest to the mirror.

Jigsaw Frames

The jigsaw type of frame began to be popular around the twenties. The idea has been carried forwarded to today as exemplified by the laminated vinyl frame previously shown.

Fig. 162. This mirror frame was made by laminating vinyl covering to plywood with a white glue. The inside edge of the frame is finished with braid.   (SUNDIAL SHADE AND GLASS CORP.)

Hobo Frames

The hobo tradition of framing comes from the latter part of the 19th century. It was so named because the materials and equipment needed to make the frames were so common. Legend has it that men traveling around the countryside made these frames to relieve their boredom.

The frames were made from soft wooden cigar boxes whittled with a simple knife. The frame was considered complete at a number of stages, from unpainted frames that carry remnants of cigar advertising on them, to painted and lacquered frames.

Fig. 163. This jigsaw frame with its many embellishments is a whimsical way to frame a mirror.(HOUSE OF H. HEYDENRYK, JR., INC.)

The hobo frame is characterized by its saw-toothed edges and over-lapping sides. Words are carved in some of the frames as shown here.

Fig. 164. Top is a frame from the Hobo tradition; bottom is a heat etched frame.

Fig. 165. Here are three designs from the Hobo tradition of framing.(HOUSE OF HEYDENRYK, JR., INC.)

Heat-Etched Frames

Another way of making a pattern in wood is to burn or scorch it. With an electric "etcher" you can burn designs and lettering, as in this frame. It was probably made in the twenties.

The basic principles of constructing a frame and its elements are fairly standard and easy to learn. If care—particularly measuring accuracy—is employed, and good equipment is used, sturdy and long lasting frames can by produced.

But there is more to successfully framing a picture. This is where artistic talent comes to the fore. The design elements, choices of molding combinations, mat texture, color and size, liners, and frame finishes—all require good taste and artistic flair. Making use of these abilities is the beginning of all the fun in framing art.

Beyond that, there is the creative drive that leads you to experiment with different equipment, fabrics and finishes that perhaps have not yet been utilized. There is deep satisfaction in experimenting; the satisfaction is compounded if the overall frame effect blends to perfection with your art. But in the beginning, remember that getting there is half the fun.

Bibliography

Barnes, Robert C.: "Uptight Clamp for All Picture Frames." *Popular Science*, 197 (1970):111.

Bauof, Ellwood and Chapin, Robert C., Jr. *Handmade Picture Frames from Simple Moldings*. Philadelphia, PA: Countryside Press, 1971.

Burnett, Janet and Laurence. *The Picture Framer's Handbook*. NY: Clarkson N. Potter, Inc., 1973.

"Classic Picture Frames." *Popular Science*, 199 (1971):84.

Murphy, Buck P.: "Proper Print Positioning." *Design*, 75 (1974):22.

Newman, Thelma R., Jay Hartley and Lee Scott. *The Frame Book*. NY: Crown Publishers, Inc., 1974.

Reinhardt, Ed and Rogers, Hal. *How to Make Your Own Picture Frames*. NY: Watson-Guptill Publications, 1958.

Sources

Aluminum Section Frame, Inc. (framer and framed art)
  429 Broome St.
  New York, NY 10013

Art Infinitum Inc. (DAX Frames)
  432 East 91st St.
  New York, NY 10028

Charles D. Burns Company (ready-made frames)
  28 Damrell St.
  Boston, MA

Greg Copeland, Inc. (art)
  41 Central Ave.
  Passaic, NJ 07055

E.I. du Pont de Nemours & Company (Corian)
  1007 Market St.
  Wilmington, DE

Betty Guy (artist)
  147 Ripley St.
  San Francisco, CA

The House of H. Heydenryk, Jr. Inc. (framers)
  417 East 76th St.
  New York, NY 10021

Jewelite Signs (Jewelite)
  13 E. 31st St.
  New York, NY 10016

Kulicke Contract (framers, ready-made frames)
  636 Broadway
  New York, NY

Julius Lowy Frame and Restoring Co., Inc. (framers)
  511 E. 72nd St.
  New York, NY 10021

Rohm & Haas (Plexiglas)
  Independence Mall West
  Philadelphia, PA

Siamese Imports Co., Inc. (papier-mâché frames)
  71 Plandome Rd.
  Manhasset, NY

Stanley Works, The (miter boxes and other tools)
  195 Lake St.
  New Britain, CT

Sundial Shade and Glass Corp. (mirrors)
  1491 First Ave.
  New York, NY 10003

Index

122

124